INFLUENCING YOUR WORLD LIKE JESUS

JEANNIE VOGEL

Dedication

To the amazing women I have met through First Steps Bible studies, Life Designs, pregnancy resource centers, neighborhood Christmas gatherings, and more. You have shown me hunger for God's truth, made me defend my faith, challenged me in practical areas of life, and often given me a glimpse of the transforming power of God to change lives. I am blessed to call you friends.

Engage: Influencing Your World like Jesus
© 2020 Regular Baptist Press • Arlington Heights, Illinois
www.RegularBaptistPress.org • 1-800-727-4440
Printed in U.S.A. All rights reserved.
RBP5527 • ISBN: 978-1-64213-677-7

Contents

An Invitation to Engage

When I was a young pastor's wife, my desire to share the gospel seemed thwarted by the reality that almost everyone in my world was a Christian. It seemed difficult to build relationships with those who didn't share my ethical, moral, or spiritual views. But I realized by studying the Gospels that this was a solvable problem. Studying Jesus' life, I noticed His friend list included many colorful characters who were nothing like Him. The key seemed to be found in Luke 19:10. Jesus didn't just come to "save" the lost; He also came to seek them.

What a difference that concept made in my life as God challenged me to find ways to engage my world. Through neighborhood Bible studies, pregnancy resource centers, Christmas gatherings, Life Design (mini workshop) breakfasts, office Bible studies, and other activities (even indoor tennis), my life has been enriched by so many women outside the normal sphere of my small Christian circle. This study is not a how-to guide on forming relationships, but it is a challenge for you to learn from Jesus how to engage your world. We are each called to reach the world for Christ and make disciples, but . . . *we will never have impact without contact.*

This study is designed to do three things:

- help you evaluate your personal relationship with Jesus;
- help you observe how Jesus engaged His world; and
- motivate you to purposefully engage a wider variety of people to influence them for Christ.

LESSON 1

An Introduction to Engage

"For the Son of Man has come to seek and to save that which was lost" (Luke 19:10).

WHILE STUDYING THE GOSPELS, I've noticed that Jesus beautifully illustrated how to establish and maintain healthy relationships. He spent hours each day interacting with a variety of people that He met in towns and villages. He noticed them, talked with them, and ate with them. He also maintained diversity in His friendships by caring as much for the social outcasts as He did for the Jewish elite. Those suffering physically boldly sought Him, yet He sought those who were ashamed to look Him in the eye and offered them hope and forgiveness. He ministered consistently to people around Him yet always took time to renew His strength through His Heavenly Father. Although Jesus left many needs unmet at His death, He was confident that He had finished the work God had given Him to do. Perhaps a closer look at Christ's life will help to put our relationships into perspective and free us to minister more effectively to the needy world around us.

A Connected Generation with Few Real Relationships

Ours could be called "the anonymous generation," because it's so easy to live solitary lives in the middle of crowds. Waiting in lines, sitting at the doctor's office, or even walking down the street could be a social event, but we often prefer to be engaged in our own private world. Phones, tablets, and earphones allow us to listen to music, read email, view social media, watch shows, or chat with friends while the world walks by us unnoticed. Even at family or church gatherings, it's not uncommon to see half the heads looking down at their screens instead of engaging people beside them. Perhaps we spend more time typing than talking because it is less intimidating than trying to connect with someone we don't know well or someone we might not see again. Regardless of the reason, too often we ignore the people who cross our path rather than really see them and engage them in conversation. And although it might be common, it poses a problem.

When we study Jesus' life on earth, we understand that He lived with a different ethos. His eyes were always open, seeing the people around Him. No one, whether hiding in a tree or concealed in a large crowd, seemed able to sneak by Jesus unnoticed. He walked with hands and heart extended to people of all walks of life, with the specific purpose of giving them hope, help, and healing. His methods were varied, but His ministry was always people centered. While His help was often tangible, His goal was always spiritual. Perhaps we need to rethink our relationships in view of Christ's perfect example.

The First Step in Relationships Is Seeing People

Jesus was a master at building relationships, because He was a master at noticing people. He observed them as they passed in and out of His life. In a boat, in a tree, in a crowd, or at a well, He was always scanning the scene for people who needed Him. Luke 19:10 states that Jesus' mission was to seek and to save those who were lost. Seeking people means we must notice them.

1. Look up the following verses and summarize the interactions Jesus had with various people.

   Matthew 4:18–20, Simon and Andrew

   Mark 10:17–22, a rich young ruler

   Luke 7:2–6, a Roman centurion

   Luke 7:11–15, a widow who lost her only son

   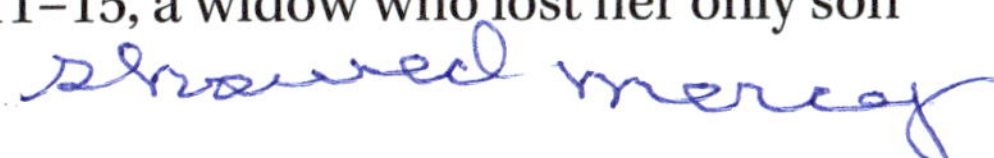

   John 4:4–10, a Samaritan woman

   John 5:2, 5–9, a lame man

Consider the variety of this group. Jesus impacted people because He connected with them in a physical way and also in a spiritual way. For most of us, maintaining relationships is an integral part of our lives. But for us Christians, relationships take on greater significance because of the task Jesus has given us.

2. Read Matthew 5:14–16.

   (a) What did Jesus say to His followers?

   (b) What can a Christian do to shine her light before others?

When Jesus mentioned that a city set on a hill cannot be hidden, He didn't mean believers should live in a fortress, high above the sinful world below. Instead we need to let our lights shine before others so they will see our good works and glorify God. But this cannot happen without relationships.

3. Read 2 Corinthians 5:18–20.

   (a) What task did God assign believers after Jesus returned to Heaven?

   (b) How should that assignment affect our relationships?

When mail carriers are given a letter to deliver, it's a crime for them to keep it for themselves. Their job is to deliver it to a certain person, which means seeking that person and delivering the letter, even if it is inconvenient or difficult. The gospel was entrusted to us in the same way: to share with others. While enjoying the comfort and blessing the gospel brings us, we often forget that we are tasked with sharing the Good News with the world.

4. Right before Jesus ascended to Heaven (Acts 1:8), what did He say to all His followers?

Most of us find it much easier to sing the old song "People Need the Lord" than to witness for the Lord. We have several reasonable, if not convincing, arguments for why we hesitate to share the gospel. Even though it's the best thing that ever happened to us, the words stick in our throats, sound forced, and make us feel insecure and unprepared. For some reason witnessing just doesn't come naturally.

Maybe it is because we forget that we should simply be introducing two people to each other—our friends and our best friend, Jesus. Our friends initially have nothing in common with Jesus except us. But their need for Him should overshadow our timidity. Imagine introducing friends with smallpox to Edward Jenner, who developed the smallpox vaccine. They might find him boring until they discover he holds the key to healing their sickness. Jesus is the universal donor that can heal everyone's sin, but He does not do so without their permission.

Or maybe it is because we have not taken the time to develop relationships with others around us to earn the privilege of sharing Christ with them. An important point to remember is that *there is no impact without contact!* If we want to make a difference in the world, we must force ourselves to engage in new relationships.

5. Read 1 Thessalonians 2:4–8, then describe how Paul and his missionary team carried out the task of sharing the gospel among the people of Thessalonica.

Paul understood the concept of sharing life with others as Jesus did. When Jesus was on earth, He spent time with many groups of people. He walked with them, talked with them, ate with them, and did life with them—regardless of whether they were sinners, outcasts, rebels, or lepers. When He met the disciples, He called them to travel with Him and go where He went. This might not be feasible in our culture, but certainly inviting people into our homes, picnicking with them in the backyard, or conversing over a cup of coffee would be sharing our lives with them.

6. How does 2 Corinthians 2:14–15 describe our impact for Christ on others?

Fragrance is interesting. It floats through the air, permeating everything around it. I have sometimes enjoyed wafts of lovely scents as I've walked by a fragrance counter or a candle store. On the other hand, I've also been assaulted by a different smell when passing a gymnasium after a basketball game. I am sure you have too. Depending on how we treat everyone, we can leave a positive or negative impression. But remember, no fragrance of our knowledge of God is left behind if we never get close enough for others to smell it.

Learning from Jesus

Studying how Jesus interacted with people in His world should make it easier for us to engage the people in ours. Have you ever stopped to think how many different relationships you experience? I am not referring only to the people who make your Christmas card list, but also the people with whom you rub shoulders daily and don't even know their names. Even if we wave to the mail carrier, greet the store salespeople with a friendly hello, and say hi to our neighbor walking her dog, these people usually remain anonymous to us. As society has become increasingly impersonal, we have learned to simply ignore those around us if they are not already in our circle of friends or family.

7. List people you see regularly or occasionally that you have not taken time to get to know.

   Name:
      Relationship:
      Role in your life:
      Place you encounter the person:

   Name:
      Relationship:
      Role in your life:
      Place you encounter the person:

   Name:
      Relationship:
      Role in your life:
      Place you encounter the person:

   Name:
      Relationship:
      Role in your life:
      Place you encounter the person:

   Name:
      Relationship:
      Role in your life:
      Place you encounter the person:

Because our lives are to reflect Christ, each person we meet provides an opportunity to impact someone for His glory. And each interaction is planned by God for a purpose. I wonder how Jesus would have reacted to the people in my world. Would He wave impersonally to the mail carrier or get to know that person's name and needs? Would He glibly ask people, "How are you doing today?" Or would He stop to find out?

Think about It

Consider these two questions this week as you think about your relationships:

1. Should I merely seek to manage relationships with the people already connected with me, or should I be seeking relationships with others with the goal of impacting them with the gospel?
2. How many people do I walk past daily without looking them in the eyes, considering their needs, or reaching out in some way?

Action Steps

1. Pray daily for the nameless people God will put in your path this week, and ask Him to allow you to connect with one new person.
2. Keep a notebook and record the people God puts in your path in various settings this week.

Verse

Memorize and think about Luke 19:10: "For the Son of Man has come to seek and to save that which was lost."

LESSON 2

The Primary Relationship

"But as it is written, 'Eye has not seen, nor ear heard, nor have entered into the heart of man the things which God has prepared for those who love Him'" (1 Corinthians 2:9).

RECENTLY A GROUP OF RESEARCHERS studied the question, What makes people happy? The surprising answer was "good relationships, especially close, positive relationships." Most people agree that the need to belong and to find intimacy with others is basic. But why is it so difficult to form and keep good relationships? Broken homes, fractured families, and splitting churches all showcase the need to improve our interaction with each other. Christian counselors Les and Leslie Parrott begin their course on relationships by saying, "If you try to find intimacy with another person before achieving a sense of wholeness on your own, all your relationships become an attempt to complete yourself."[1]

Before you try to understand any of your relationships, you need to understand your own identity and purpose. As Elisabeth Elliot said, "You can't make proper use of something unless you know what it was made for."[2] So the first step in improving our relationships with others is to determine our purpose in life by analyzing why we were created. Then we can understand the purpose of our other relationships.

Back to the Beginning

Read Genesis 1:24–27; 2:7–17.

1. Contrast the creation of animals with the creation of mankind.

2. According to Genesis 1:27–30, how did God's relationship with Adam differ from His relationship with the animals and other creatures?

3. Describe the details given about God's relationship with mankind. Finish the sentences I started below.

   Genesis 2:7—God formed man and

   Genesis 2:8–9—God gave man a

   Genesis 2:15—God assigned man to tend and

   Genesis 2:16–17—God commanded man

   Genesis 2:18–22—God made woman and brought her to Adam as his

It is obvious from these verses that God took care of all Adam's needs. The Lord provided food, protection, meaningful work, and a perfect relationship.

> "When I consider Your heavens, the work of Your fingers, the moon and the stars, which You have ordained, what is man that You are mindful of him, and the son of man that You visit him? For You have made him a little lower than the angels, and you have crowned him with glory and honor. You have made him to have dominion over the works of Your hands; You have put all things under his feet." (Psalm 8:3–6)

The Purpose of Creating Mankind

4. Look at these New Testament passages to determine some of the reasons God chose to create mankind, then write down those reasons:

   Ephesians 1:4–6

   Ephesians 1:11–12

   Ephesians 2:10

   Read Genesis 2:8–9; 15–17.

5. Based on Adam's original duties, how would Adam's work in the Garden initially reflect God's purpose for him?

In Genesis 2:18, God shows a special compassion for Adam. After He declared that it was not good that man should be alone, God chose to create a companion who could form a human relationship with Adam.

6. Look carefully at Genesis 2:21–22.
   (a) What was the first relationship that the woman experienced?
   (b) What was the second relationship?

We often focus on the relationship between Adam and Eve, which is also introduced in Genesis 2, but both the man's and the woman's initial relationships were with their Creator. God formed man's body and then personally breathed His own breath into that shell of a body. At that moment, a lump of clay was transformed into a living person, who was not only different from the animals, but was in God's image. Eve was also created by God in a unique way. Both Adam and Eve had intellect, will, emotion, and the freedom to exercise those characteristics. The God of the universe spent time with them and talked to them in a personal way. So, from their first steps on the earth, humans had the privilege of a personal relationship with Almighty God, their Creator and friend.

A New Relationship

When God brought Eve to Adam, He introduced humans to a new type of relationship. Although God introduced this concept of union between man and woman as a permanent relationship, it was never to be in competition with His unique relationship to each of them. His primary relationship to them as their creator and sustainer was to remain their most important relationship. Together they were to bring God glory.

A Broken Relationship

Read Genesis 3:1–13.

7. According to Genesis 3:1–5, what methods did Satan use to undermine God's relationship with Eve?

When Eve listened to Satan, she fell victim to lies that derailed her relationship with God. She doubted God and misrepresented His words. But the underlying reason she yielded to temptation was dissatisfaction with how she was created. Rather than embrace her created role, she wanted to be like God. This is a trap that women fall into to this day by refusing to accept the role God created us to fulfill. Romans 9:20 says, "O man, who are you to reply against God? Will the thing formed say to him who formed it, 'Why have you made me like this?'"

8. Reread Genesis 3:7–13. Explain the result of this rift in man's relationship with God and how it also affected Adam and Eve's relationship with each other.

These first three short chapters in Genesis record how the wonderful relationship between God and man was established, then smashed. As Creator, God designed Adam and Eve to enjoy a close, personal relationship with Him and bring Him glory and praise. Nothing indicates how long this special relationship existed between God and Adam and Eve, but it came to a screeching halt in one day because the couple allowed someone to come between them and God. He, as Creator, had every right to give the orders, set the rules, and be in charge. But when Satan appealed to human pride and encouraged Adam and Eve to challenge the perfect relationship they had always enjoyed with God, they learned for the first time what it means to be without

God. By choosing to forsake that relationship, they also forsook the wisdom of God, the communion with God, and the benefits that God provided in the Garden. The saddest part of this passage is the indication that never again on this earth would anyone enjoy the perfect relationship that God had first established with Adam and Eve.

A Broken World

9. Read Romans 5:12 and 1 Corinthians 15:21–22. What do these New Testament verses say about the effect of Adam's sin on humanity?

10. Read the following verses. In each passage, how does God describe those who are without Him?

    Romans 3:10–18

    Romans 5:6, 10

    Ephesians 2:12

11. Romans 1:18–21 explains that because of sin, people are separated from God and under His wrath. What evidence do these verses present that no one can exclusively blame Adam and Eve for his or her own lack of relationship with God?

Romans 1 describes mankind's progression of rejecting not only a relationship with God but, eventually, the existence of God Himself. Verse 28 says, "And even as they did not like to retain God in their knowledge, God gave them over to a debased mind, to do those things which are not fitting." No one can fulfill the purpose for which he or she was created while remaining ungodly, an enemy of God. A broken relationship with God not only thwarts the purpose for which we were created but also wreaks havoc on our relational ability with others.

12. Read Romans 1:28–31.
    (a) What descriptions of sinners stem from a broken relationship with God?

    (b) How do these character flaws hurt human relationships?

How to Reestablish a Relationship with God

It is obvious that any study of relationships must start with an understanding of how to reestablish and maintain a personal relationship with the Creator, God. This essential relationship will bring meaning and purpose to our lives and give us direction in other relationships.

13. According to the following verses, what part does Jesus play in reestablishing our relationship with God? What is our part?

    John 3:16–18
        Jesus' part
        Our part

    Romans 5:8–10
        Jesus' part
        Our part

    Romans 10:9–10
        God's part
        Our part

14. Read the following verses, then describe the benefits of believers, who have been restored to Creator God.

    Hebrews 7:25

    Colossians 1:13–14

    1 Peter 2:9–10

> "What shall I render to the Lord for all His benefits toward me?" (Psalm 116:12)

Every relationship takes time and effort. A relationship with God is no different. Time spent studying the Bible and getting to know God shouldn't be obligatory but should flow from love and gratitude for what God has accomplished for you. Good relationships are based on love and commitment. When we consider God's care for us—from creation to redemption through the death of His Son, Jesus Christ—we realize what a great debt we owe to His love and grace.

The Results of Our Relationship with God

Our relationship with God will have a direct effect on our relationships with others. According to Philippians 2, when we share the mind of Christ, we will put the interest of others ahead of our own.

15. Read the following verses and identify the instructions that, if followed, could change our human relationships.

    Romans 12:9–21

Galatians 5:22–26

Matthew 5:43–44

16. Read 2 Corinthians 5:14–15. What overarching motivation should drive those who have a renewed relationship with God?

Relationships are an essential component of life. Scripture teaches that a personal relationship with God is essential to understanding our own identity and purpose and is foundational for maintaining good relationships with others. Without God, we cannot grasp how relationships should function, and we do not have the capability to set aside our selfish agendas and seek the good of others. God's supernatural grace and power in us transform ungodly humans into His spiritual servants. So if you are serious about allowing God to transform your relationships, start by reevaluating your personal relationship with God Himself.

Think about It

Ponder these two questions this week as you think about your relationships:

1. Was there a specific time when you put your faith in Jesus Christ as your personal Savior from sin and renewed the broken relationship with God? If not, do not put off making this commitment today.
2. Do your relationships with others reflect the power of God working through you?

Action Steps

1. Write one personal goal for this week that will help you draw closer to God.

2. Choose one or two of the Biblical instructions from question 15. Ask God to help you implement that instruction this week so His character will reflect in your life and relationships.

Verse

Memorize and think about 1 Corinthians 2:9: "But as it is written, 'Eye has not seen, nor ear heard, nor have entered into the heart of man the things which God has prepared for those who love Him.'"

Endnotes

[1]Les Parrott and Leslie Parrott, "The Single Sentence That Can Change Your Relationships" in "Devotion: Loving God and Each Other," *Les + Leslie Parrott*, https://www.lesandleslie.com/devotions/the-single-sentence.

[2]Elisabeth Elliot, *Let Me Be a Woman* (Wheaton: Tyndale House Publishers, 1982), 22.

LESSON 3

The Original Tie That Binds

"But if anyone does not provide for his own [relatives], and especially for those of his household, he has denied the faith and is worse than an unbeliever" (1 Timothy 5:8).

BE HONEST. HAVE YOU EVER SKIPPED over a long list of Biblical genealogies? They list name after name, usually mentioning only the father but occasionally listing the mother as well. It is hard to remember that each of these names represents a real family, just like the ones in your neighborhood. They had cute, cuddly babies with names like Ashkenaz, Riphath, and Togarmah, who would carry on their line.

Hidden inside boring "begats" are stories of families that experienced joys, sorrows, lies, pain, hurt, happiness, and hope. The Bible doesn't gloss over family problems but rather exposes the secrets, like Mr. and Mrs. Abraham's problems with trust, leadership, and jealousy or Mr. and Mrs. Isaac's problems of deceit and betrayal. Despite problems, the Bible holds the family up as an irreplaceable unit established to be permanent and productive. God chose to place His own Son into a human family, rather than have Him appear as a ruler and king. Though little is written about Jesus as a child, we can learn important principles about family relationships by studying His life.

Families Were Established by God in the Beginning

Family relationships represent the oldest human relationship. Some say dogs are man's best friend, but when each animal paraded before Adam in Genesis 1:26–29, he was still missing a mutually fulfilling relationship. It wasn't until God brought Eve to Adam, introducing the idea of human relationship, that Adam found true companionship. Eve was created in the image of God, and although she was different physiologically, she was like Adam. It was God, not Adam or Eve, Who presented the idea of marriage and family, as indicated by Genesis 2:24.

1. Read Genesis 2:24–25. What words are used to express the unity and commitment between Adam and Eve?

2. Read Genesis 1:27–31. Which responsibilities were given to both Adam and Eve?

God introduced the concept of union between man and woman as a permanent relationship. One man and one woman were to function as a unit to fulfill the mandate from God. In Genesis 3 Adam and Eve disobeyed God, and sin marred their relationship with Him and each other. In Genesis 4 they began to "multiply and fill the earth." Soon the first family suffered from sin, when their firstborn son, Cain, murdered his brother Abel. Adam's family was the first of many dysfunctional families noted in the Bible. Historical accounts of families with sinful problems abound throughout its pages.

No Families Are Perfect—Not Even Jesus' Family

3. Read Matthew 1, noting who was in Jesus' family tree. Name some family problems of people in His lineage.

   Abraham (Genesis 20:1–2)

   Jacob (Genesis 27:19–29, 41)

   Tamar (Genesis 38:6, 11–18, 24–26)

   Rahab (Joshua 2:1; 6:23)

   David (2 Samuel 11:2–5)

Murder, incest, lying, cheating, hate, immorality, deceit—it's all there. Are you surprised at the stories of deviancy in Jesus' family tree? We might disown these relatives, but God chose this dysfunctional heritage for His Son. God obviously was not looking for a perfect family. He placed His perfect Son into a messy family line, because Jesus came to seek and save messed up lives (Luke 19:10). This should remind us that instead of being embarrassed by our family imperfections, we can see how God can change and use us too.

Jesus and His Earthly Family

Although not everyone in Mary's lineage was pure, she had a different résumé.

4. What can we learn from Luke 1:26–30 about Mary, who was chosen to be the mother of Jesus?

5. Read Luke 1:31–38. Given all the unknowns of her situation, how does Mary's response to the angel's announcement showcase her faith in God?

6. In Luke 1:46–55 how does Mary's song of praise imply her knowledge of God and His work?

The Bible does not reveal many details about Jesus' childhood except that He grew up in the family of Mary and Joseph. Since Jesus had a divine Father, no human father was necessary. But God chose Joseph as a surrogate father for Jesus, to provide for Him and protect Him.

7. Read Matthew 1:18–25. How did Joseph show his faith in God after hearing the angel's message?

8. According to Matthew 2:13–15, how did Joseph protect Jesus when He was a baby?

9. Why was it important that Jesus' family listened to and obeyed God? See Matthew 2:19–23.

Although Mary and Joseph were godly people, following God's commands in a sinful world was no easier in the first century than it is today. Jesus' parents made a priority of following the Mosaic law. They took Jesus to be circumcised, then later traveled from Bethlehem to Jerusalem to present Him to the Lord and offer their sacrifice. Finally, they trekked back to their hometown of Nazareth with Him. Luke 2:41 relates that each year they made the trip back to Jerusalem for the Feast of the Passover. On one of these trips, when Jesus was twelve, they accidently left Him in Jerusalem because He was talking with teachers in the temple.

10. Read Luke 2:43–50. How did Jesus respond to His family after being questioned by His mother?

11. Read Luke 2:51–52. How did Jesus show respect to His earthly family even after He had begun taking care of His Heavenly Father's business?

Many people try to deemphasize or redefine traditional mother-and-father families, but God placed Jesus into a home with a mother and a father. Jesus submitted to their leadership and care in this setting. He grew in areas of wisdom, stature, and favor with God and man. His life showed that even a sinless child must show respect and honor to His parents. Their authority was not given on the basis of their moral superiority but on the basis of their God-given roles and responsibilities. Mary and Joseph weren't perfect parents, because they weren't perfect people, but God chose them to raise Jesus in a godly atmosphere. But not all their children responded the same.

Jesus and His Brothers

Jesus also grew up with siblings, which is, some might say, the ultimate test of spirituality. Unlike earthly siblings, all the wrongs done against Jesus, even when He was a child, were unwarranted and unfair. He never deserved mistreatment, because He never sinned. But the Bible never records an outburst from Jesus about injustice, nor does it display Jesus with a victim mentality. Neither does the Bible record Jesus in active public ministry until age thirty. So it appears that thirty of His thirty-three years on earth were spent with His natural family. Yet even His own brothers did not at first believe He was the Messiah.

12. Read John 2:1–5.

    (a) Who was present at Jesus' first earthly miracle?

    (b) Who originally traveled with Jesus, according to John 2:11–12?

13. Read Mark 3:21.

    (a) How did Jesus' family respond to His teaching and casting out demons?

    (b) Read John 7:3–5. How did His brothers respond to Jesus' teaching?

Primary Relationships Are Those That No One Else Can Fulfill

It must have been painful to Jesus to experience His brothers' rebuke and rejection. Since sin entered the world, all relationships have suffered, and Jesus' family was not exempt.

Sometimes relationships with family will be difficult or exhausting or frustrating or maybe even seem impossible. Just as God put Jesus into a family tree with many problems, God has placed each of us into a family of sinners. But marriage and family remain important to God, Who initiated them. First Timothy 5:8 spells out the priority of caring for family regardless of the relationship: "But if anyone does not provide for his relatives, and especially for members of his household, he has denied the faith and is worse than an unbeliever."

If family is to be a priority, then each relationship must also be important. Since a husband or wife has only one spouse, no one else can legitimately meet the wife's or the husband's needs if the marital relationship is neglected. Children have only one mother, so if she neglects her responsibility to that primary relationship, the children will suffer. Just as the Mosaic law commanded children to obey their parents, Jesus spoke strongly about adult children's relationships to their mothers and fathers. Sometimes adult children are the only ones able to care for an aging parent. This becomes a primary relationship, since Scripture says we are to honor our parents.

14. Why did Jesus rebuke the Pharisees in Matthew 15:1–9?

15. Read John 19:25–27. How did Jesus show care for His mother at His death?

An Invitation to a New Family

From the beginning Jesus knew He had two families, which is why even at twelve years old, He was doing His Father's work. When Jesus began His public ministry, His priority shifted to His Heavenly Father's family.

16. Read Luke 8:19–21. How do these verses show a change in Jesus' priority?

17. Read Matthew 10:37. What is the one priority that should be more important to us than family?

While we are studying the strong Biblical emphasis on family, we must acknowledge that the topic of family can bring pain, anger, and remorse, because sometimes families abuse, abandon, ignore, and betray each other. I had an amazing and godly birth family, but as a parent of some prodigals, for me the mention of family sometimes brings up discouragement, disappointment, and even guilt that comes when those you love reject God's truth.

However, the subject of family should bring joy to every believer, because one of the most beautiful Biblical truths is that Jesus allows anyone to join His forever family. Galatians 4:4 says, "But when the fullness of time had come, God sent forth His Son, born of a woman, born under the law, to redeem those who were under the law, that we might receive the adoption as sons." Titus 3:4–5 explains that because of God's goodness and loving kindness, He includes us in His family even though we have done nothing to deserve it.

18. According to Titus 3:4–7, what benefits do we receive as God's children?

Instead of focusing on our earthly family, who may hurt or disappoint us unjustly, we can always rejoice that our Heavenly Father does not treat us as our sins deserve but instead gives us the love, forgiveness, eternal home, and inheritance we do not deserve.

Importance of Family

Here are three summary principles about family given in Scripture:

First, we must avoid the temptation to ignore the mundane responsibilities of family to engage in more exciting activities, including work or even ministries in the church. Seeing God's view of family and the priority for placing Jesus into a family should help us grasp the importance of our family unit and encourage us to make it a priority.

Second, we should not love our families more than we love God Himself, which can happen if we are consumed with earthly goals and material gains for our families.

Third, being adopted into God's perfect family gives us joy, hope, and blessings regardless of the state of our earthly families.

Think about It

Think about these six statements this week as you work on your relationships:

1. Our heritage does not define our future usefulness or holiness.
2. God chose a sinful family for Jesus' entrance into the world.
3. Jesus took His responsibility to His family seriously.
4. God understands that families aren't perfect, yet He emphasizes their importance.
5. Our relationship to God has ultimate priority.
6. God provides a perfect family to all who believe in His Son.

Action Steps

1. Make a list of your family members and prioritize which ones need your attention most, because no one else can fulfill your role in their lives.

2. Now mark those that are primary and exclusive with a *P*. Plan how you will invest in those lives. Make sure to schedule time for them in your weekly planner.
3. Acknowledge whether your earthly family helped or hindered your spiritual growth. Accept that God placed you in that family for a reason.
4. Make sure you are in God's family through belief in His Son, Jesus (John 1:12; Galatians 3:23–26).

Verse

Memorize and think about 1 Timothy 5:8: "But if anyone does not provide for his own [relatives], and especially for members of his household, he has denied the faith and is worse than an unbeliever."

LESSON 4

Invest in People, Not Things

"And you became followers of us and of the Lord, having received the word in much affliction, with joy of the Holy Spirit" (1 Thessalonians 1:6).

HAVE YOU EVER CONSIDERED the purpose of friendships? Are most friendships for support, laughs, camaraderie, spiritual accountability, or just common interest? On earth Jesus didn't choose disciples because they laughed at His jokes or liked similar activities. He selected them not because they would help and encourage Him but because He wanted to train them to help and encourage others. He knew their potential, which was critical to His mission in the world. He developed His closest friendships with these men and mentored them into the influencers He knew they could become.

Some might call disciples co-laborers instead of friends. Leaders looking for ministry workers look for potential in others, then mentor and help them grow. Perhaps friends and co-laborers should not be mutually exclusive. Have you ever thought about friends as missional relationships? Studying how Jesus interacted with friends might impact how you choose and relate to your closest friends.

Many Disciples Followed Jesus

Jesus' disciples were friends, comrades, and protégés who would be entrusted with the most important message ever given to mankind. The Greek word for *disciple,* which means "a learner or pupil," is used over 250 times in the Bible.

1. According to Luke 6:12–13, 17, how do we know Jesus had more than twelve disciples?

2. According to John 6:60–68, how did the disciples differ in their commitment to Jesus?

The Bible offers only glimpses of this larger group, but those glimpses prove that Jesus allowed many people into His circle of friends. These men and women followed Him because they wanted to learn more about Him, even though some eventually fell away.

Jesus Spent Time Teaching All His Disciples

Jesus purposefully taught His disciples in formal and informal settings. Before the Sermon on the Mount, Scripture says, "And seeing the multitudes, He went up on a mountain, and when He was seated His disciples came to Him. Then He opened His mouth and taught them, saying" (Matthew 5:1–2). His purpose was to teach and clarify truth but also to pass on His heart for the world.

3. What important principles did Jesus address in Matthew 5:10–19? Name three.

Jesus also taught about giving, prayer, hypocrisy, materialism, trusting God, worry, judging others, and, most importantly, that not everyone who claims to be a disciple is one. He taught the disciples true spiritual living by continually explaining that their hearts mattered as much as their outward actions. This is a very hard principle to convey, since humans can see only external evidences of the heart, but Jesus constantly communicated it to His disciples.

4. Read John 8:31 and 13:35. How did Jesus distinguish between true disciples and mere followers?

Jesus Chose Some to Have a Closer Relationship

Quite early in His ministry, Jesus chose twelve men out of the pool of disciples to have a unique relationship with Him. We call them the Twelve and the apostles. Jesus personally poured His life and message into these men of various backgrounds, temperaments, occupations, and political persuasions.

5. Read Matthew 10:2–5 and Luke 6:14–16. Record the name of each apostle and any information given about him.

Simon (not Peter) belonged to a group of Jews called Zealots, who so rigorously adhered to the Mosaic law that they sometimes resorted to violence to prevent anyone from violating laws. Then—at the opposite extreme—there was Matthew. Imagine the scene when Jesus chose him, a traitorous tax collecting Jew who worked with Rome. But most shocking is that Jesus chose Judas, knowing he was a betrayer. While the men probably kept their eyes on Matthew, Judas was stealing money and plotting Jesus' death.

Jesus Allowed the Disciples to Do Life with Him

Jesus allowed His disciples into His personal life. Too often ministry is separated from everyday living. It's easy to become hypocritical if we try to preserve a spiritual façade in front of people that doesn't reflect our real lives. Jesus walked and talked with His disciples so they would see truth in action in everyday life. Along dusty trails they heard Him speak, saw Him heal, and observed how He dealt with a variety of people. Disciples traveled and ate with Him, so they not only heard His words but observed His priorities and sometimes understood His heart. Jesus was on a mission to seek and save the lost, and by revealing His life to them, He trained His disciples to do the same.

6. According to Mark 4:33–34, how did Jesus treat His disciples differently than others?

7. In Mark 9:30–31 why didn't Jesus want others to know where He was going?

8. Read Matthew 10:1. What powers did Jesus grant to the Twelve to share His work on earth?

Jesus sent the disciples out instead of keeping them close for personal comfort. Sometimes we might be tempted to try to discourage close friends from leaving us, even to do God's will. But Jesus' goal was that they would grow and go. He didn't worry that they were not as gifted as He was. He taught them to depend on God to empower them. They were not competition to but multiplication of His ministry.

Jesus Chose to Use Weak, Sinful Men for a Great Purpose

The Gospels clearly reveal that the disciples weren't perfect and didn't always share Jesus' perspective. For example, they tried to turn away children from Him (Matthew 19). And Thomas doubted (John 20:26–29). Jesus identified three disciples—Peter, James, and John—to have an even closer relationship with Him, but even these men disappointed Him and misunderstood Him. James and John coveted supreme spots in the kingdom (20:21), and Peter denied Jesus (Matthew 26:69–75).

9. After Peter confessed that Jesus is "the Christ, the Son of the living God" in Matthew 16:16, what mistake did he make (vv. 21–23)?

10. In Mark 14:34–37 how did Jesus' closest disciples let Him down?

11. At what point in Jesus' life did all His disciples forsake Him, according to Matthew 26:55–57?

We wouldn't choose these people for friends, much less choose them to impact the world. Yet Jesus was not deterred by the apostles' human frailties. He knew the Holy Spirit would empower them to complete His work. He was not looking for born leaders, but rather men who would be transformed and used by God.

Jesus Was Honest about Their Weaknesses

It's hard to imagine how Jesus motivated these men to become leaders in three short years. He was a true friend. Without writing people off, He addressed issues, correcting Peter candidly when he misunderstood the purpose of Jesus' death, and setting James and John straight about the need for humility over pride.

We need people who are close enough (and brave enough) to help us see our own weaknesses, which, although nearly invisible to us, are usually glaring to those around us. Enemies might complain about and criticize us to others, but only a friend speaking the truth in love will honestly address our blind spots in a way that can pierce our defenses. By holding up the mirror of God's Word, friends help us recognize our sin without pretext. They encourage us to come clean in areas no one else knows are dirty. They encourage us to grow no matter how little or how much we have grown already.

12. What does Proverbs 27:17 say about the benefit of a good friend?

13. How have you experienced this type of friendship?

Jesus Understood That His Disciples Were Sinners

Jesus wasn't surprised that one of His closest friends and disciples eventually betrayed Him, but we are always surprised if it happens to us. We are hurt, upset, and angry, and we cannot understand the betrayal. Why?

We expect our closest friends to be beyond failure. We want them to act more like Jesus than like us. However, only one person in history was sinless, and He no longer lives on earth. Jesus always knew that His most spiritual, loyal friend was still a sinful human and could fail. Only Jesus will never fail. So prepare to work with fallible humans the rest of your life.

Unfortunately, we're tempted to avoid people if they might let us down. But in Scripture Jesus repeatedly said we need one another. He also demonstrated that truth by His connection to His disciples. We are commanded to stay close and not try to stand alone. Instead, like Jesus, we are to take our hurts to God and ask for His will to be done, then continue serving beside the same people. We are to accept people's failures, as they accept ours.

Two Types of Betrayal

Read Matthew 26:30–75.

14. In Matthew 26:33–35, what did Peter boast about in respect to his commitment to Jesus?

15. According to Matthew 26:69–75, how did Peter respond when he realized how he had failed Jesus?

A friend's betrayal is never easy and must have been painful for Jesus in His darkest hour. But after Peter's remorse, Jesus trusted him to lead His flock again. It wasn't Peter's failure but his response to failure to which Jesus responded. Jesus saw potential in Peter and wouldn't let personal disappointment hinder forgiveness. Peter was a true disciple who went horribly astray but was repentant and forgiven. Even close spiritual friends will sometimes let us down. It's difficult to let them be reinstated, but based on Jesus' example, we can learn to forgive. Like Jesus, we can also challenge them to be faithful in the future.

16. Read Matthew 26:14–16. What deal did Judas make with the chief priests?

17. According to Luke 22:47–48, how did Jesus react to His disciple's betrayal?

18. Read Matthew 27:3–5. What was Judas's final response to his deed?

Jesus knew that Judas would betray Him, yet He allowed Judas to be on His ministry team. Jesus understood that Satan would use Judas to condemn Him to death and that Judas would never repent. Jesus also knew that we, too, will face traitors, so He set an example in His gracious treatment of Judas.

Right before Judas betrayed Jesus and Peter denied Him, Jesus tied a towel around His waist and washed their feet (John 13:3–5). He served and loved those who would betray and deny Him, just as He did those who loved Him. He also spent time praying for all of them.

19. Read John 13:14–15. What is significant about Jesus' message to the men after He washed their feet?

Jesus' Disciples Grew Stronger after He Left

One of the greatest miracles recorded in the Bible is the transformation of Jesus' unruly, untrained, and uneducated disciples, who received power from the Holy Spirit and turned the world upside down.

20. Compare how Peter responded during Jesus' initial arrest with how he responded when he was arrested in Acts 5:18–20, 27–32.

The disciples, once a fearful, doubting group, stood publicly and fearlessly declaring the truth of Jesus' death and resurrection. They lived courageously in the face of persecution and public disdain, and most of them died martyrs. After Jesus' ascension, they remembered the truths they had learned and practiced them. This type of commitment and change in these men did not come naturally but supernaturally. Mark 13:11 says, "But when they arrest you and deliver you up, do not worry beforehand, or premeditate what you will speak. But whatever is given you in that hour, speak that; for it is not you who speak, but the Holy Spirit."

When Jesus left His band of bewildered disciples staring up at the sky, He had given them many instructions. But the disciples were not just to preach; they were to love one another and encourage one another as His Body. Jesus knew that the disciples would need help to carry out these commands. John 14:26 says that when Jesus left earth, God would send a Helper. The fruit of that Helper (the Spirit) in them reflected Jesus' love, joy, peace, and other characteristics that were uncommon for that group of men. That is the only possible way to account for the change in these men's lives and commitment. That same Helper is available to every believer today to help us maintain godly, selfless relationships within the Body of Christ. And Jesus said that others would know they were His disciples by their love for one another.

Principles from Jesus with His Disciples

- Jesus was honest with friends about weaknesses.
- Jesus understood that even close friends fail.
- Jesus spent extra time to develop close relationships with friends.

- Jesus did not permanently write off people who failed.
- Jesus held out forgiveness and mercy even to those He knew wouldn't repent.
- Jesus expected His disciples to love each other and carry on His mission together through the power of the Holy Spirit.

Think about It

Here are three truths to ponder this week as you think about your relationships:

1. Every relationship should be missional because we should be focused on the mission Jesus laid out for us. When we follow God, people should be following us as we follow Him.
2. We don't learn just from the perfect example of Jesus Christ. We learn from flawed men like the disciples. Time spent with people means they will see our flaws but see how we repent also.
3. Beware of being so dependent on close friends that you fear speaking truth into their lives. Close relationships geared for spiritual growth will demand honesty and speaking the truth in love at times.

Action Steps

1. Give permission to a close friend to address areas of weakness she sees in your life. If she does, thank her rather than being offended.
2. Open your life to someone to share your real life—your struggles as well as joys, fears as well as faith, and pain as well as triumph.

Verse

Memorize and think about 1 Thessalonians 1:6: "And you became followers of us and of the Lord, having received the word in much affliction, with the joy of the Holy Spirit."

LESSON 5

Friends, Romans, and Pharisees

"But love your enemies, do good, and lend, hoping for nothing in return; and your reward will be great, and you will be sons of the Most High. For He is kind to the unthankful and evil" (Luke 6:35).

OUT OF ALL THE RELATIONSHIPS we experience, there is one group we do not seek, yet they show up spontaneously. They will find you whether you are young or old, rich or poor, successful or struggling. Although they are not friends, they often stick "closer than a brother." Critics come crashing into our world with harsh words, pointed fingers, and conflicting opinions, making life miserable. Almost everyone has them, but we don't always know how to treat them.

The surprising fact is that Jesus, the perfect Son of God, had critics surrounding Him too. By studying the Gospels, we can learn important lessons about why groups criticized Jesus, how He responded, and reasons for us to endure unjust treatment by critics.

Jesus Had Critics

Early in Jesus' ministry certain groups of people opposed His message. The Pharisees, men known for strict observance of the law, were some of Jesus' most vehement critics. The scribes, sometimes referred to as teachers of the law, also found fault with Him regularly. These two groups followed Jesus mercilessly throughout His earthly ministry and, although He was perfect, found plenty to criticize.

1. Read the following verses. What things did the Pharisees and scribes criticize Jesus for doing?

   Luke 5:29–30; 15:1–2

   John 5:5–9; 15–17

   Matthew 12:22–24

None of these actions seem like true offenses, but Jesus' critics refused to believe the truth about His deity. Luke 5 records the account of friends bringing a paralyzed man to Jesus and lowering him through the roof to be healed. Verse 20 says, "When He saw their faith, He said to him, 'Man, your sins are forgiven you.'"

2. Read Luke 5:21. How did the scribes and Pharisees respond?

3. Read Luke 5:22–26. How did Jesus back up His claim to deity?

When the man walked, people watching, including some scribes and Pharisees, were amazed and glorified God (v. 26). But apparently the critics in the group were not permanently convinced of Jesus' deity.

4. How does Luke 6:6–11 reveal the heart of the scribes and Pharisees?

Over and over Jesus proved His deity by healing people, but His critics had already chosen what they would and would not believe.

Matthew 21:15 records an interesting account of Jesus in the temple. "Then the blind and the lame came to Him in the temple, and He healed them. But when the chief priests and scribes saw the wonderful things that He did, . . . they were. . . . " Reading this account, you might think the chief priests and scribes were amazed or happy or at least impressed.

5. Read Matthew 21:15. What word describes how the scribes and Pharisees responded to Jesus' miracles?

How could such a great event spawn this reply? Critics see events through a lens that colors every event with a negative hue. Jesus' critics didn't seek truth; they sought a way to silence Him.

6. Read Luke 20:22–26. Why did the Pharisees ask Jesus a question?

7. How did Jesus answer their question without falling into their trap?

No matter what Jesus did, His enemies were against Him. John 11 recounts Jesus' raising Lazarus to life three days after he died. People were amazed at this miracle, and news spread through the region.

8. Read John 11:45–53.
   (a) How did the Pharisees respond to Jesus' power over death?

   (b) What were their reasons?

Jesus' Truth Sometimes Offended His Critics

When Pharisees complained about Jesus' disciples breaking handwashing rules, He pointed out their inconsistency. In Matthew 15:1–13 Jesus countered that Pharisees broke the command of God for the sake of their tradition. He pointed out that their rule about keeping money to honor the Lord was a ruse to avoid supporting their parents as the law directed. He called them hypocrites and said, "These people honor me with their lips, but their hearts are far from me" (Matthew 15:8, NIV). The disciples reprimanded Jesus, saying, "Do you know the Pharisees were offended?" They questioned speaking harsh truth to these religious leaders and seemed to criticize Jesus' tactics.

9. In Matthew 15:12–14, how did Jesus respond concerning the Pharisees?

10. Read Matthew 15:17–20. While the Pharisees focused on handwashing, what did Jesus say is the true cause of defilement?

People need to be warned about critics who masquerade as spiritual leaders and lead people astray. After seeing Jesus' compassion and kindness, it probably shocked the disciples to hear Jesus' strong rebuke. Sometimes speaking the truth (even in love) will offend people who have rejected truth. In this case, Jesus needed to warn His followers about the false ideas Pharisees were promoting. Jesus strongly condemned many of this group's errors.

11. Paraphrase the statements regarding the scribes and Pharisees that Jesus makes in the following verses of Matthew 23.

    Matthew 23:3–5

    Matthew 23:6–7

    Matthew 23:23

    Matthew 23:25–26

    Matthew 23:27–28

Note that Jesus condemned the false teaching and hypocritical lifestyle of these religious leaders, not in retaliation for their treatment of Him, but to make sure people were not led astray by would-be Biblical scholars. Similarly today a false narrative about Jesus has become popular, teaching that because Jesus is love, He will not condemn ungodly actions, beliefs, or teachings. These passages in Matthew 23 reveal that nothing could be further from the truth. Jesus was blunt about unbiblical behavior and was willing to challenge those who promoted it.

Sometimes Critics Seem to Be Winning

Jewish leaders manipulated circumstances so Jesus was killed by the Romans, because as the Jews admit in John 18:31, "It is unlawful for us to put anyone to death." John 18:28 records that Jews led Jesus from the house of Caiaphas to the palace of the Roman governor but refused to enter. They wanted to avoid ceremonial uncleanness that morning so they could eat the Passover meal. Imagine the irony of sending the Perfect Lamb of God to be killed, then celebrating Passover by eating a lamb representing redemption from death.

Critics Love Company

I've noticed an interesting fact about critical people—whether in families, churches, or politics. Critics love to have someone agree with them about their intended target. Finding a comrade who scorns the same individual gives the two a bond of sorts. Perhaps it helps them share negative information, legitimatizes their concerns, or even helps them justify their behavior. But sometimes critics have nothing in common except hating their target. This was certainly true of Jesus' critics. At the end of His life, the group that planned His death was an unlikely one.

12. Who conspired to convict and kill Jesus, according to Luke 22:1–6, 66–71?

13. Compare Luke 23:1–2 with Matthew 22:21. What lies did the conspirators spread about Jesus?

14. According to Luke 23:10–11, 22–24, whom did the religious Jews partner with to kill Jesus?

15. Considering the Jews' relationship with Rome during these years, what is unusual about the statement the Jews made in John 19:12?

It is interesting to note that some of the people who hated each other were willing to work together to put Jesus to death. Their goal had nothing to do with Caesar. They simply used the Roman government as a cover for their murderous intent.

We Can Benefit and Learn from Critics

The purpose of enduring suffering at the hands of critics

While none of the criticisms leveled against Jesus were legitimate, it is important to recognize that although not all criticisms against us are legitimate either, they might still have an important purpose.

16. Read Matthew 16:21. Why did Jesus tolerate abuse from His critics when He could have prevented it?

Jesus showed an unswerving trust in the sovereignty of God. The Father allowed Jesus' suffering at the hands of His enemies to accomplish the redemption of mankind, including the redemption of those very men who mocked, jeered, and put Him to death. Jesus ultimately suffered at the hand of His critics to save those critics (and others) from the penalty of their sin.

Critics may tell the truth

In this study of how Jesus dealt with His critics and enemies, one important point needs to be made. Jesus never deserved any of the criticism He received. He lived a perfect life and never disobeyed the Father. We know this isn't true of us. So the first thing to do when critics condemn us, and they will, is to listen to them and then analyze their complaints. Even though critics might approach topics in a callous manner, they might share a kernel of truth that is important to hear. God might use them to point out an area of weakness or error that our friends won't identify.

17. What is your typical response to criticism?

Critics Can Help Refine Us

Whether justified or not, the suffering we endure at the hands of critics always has a purpose in the sovereignty of God. It might be to determine if we are serving for the glory of God or man. It might help us learn whether we display the fruit of the Spirit under pressure. It might be to test our faith in God's goodness. It might be for unbelievers to see whether our response is Biblical.

Wrong reactions to criticism make us question God's purposes or feel we are treated unfairly. By responding with retaliation or complaint, we short-circuit God's process of purifying us through these trials. But if we allow ourselves to be led by the Father's will, as Jesus did, we will have the strength not only to endure but also to respond in a way that glorifies God.

Critics Are to Be Prayed for, Loved, and Forgiven

One of the most important lessons about critics can be seen in Jesus' ultimate response to them. Although Jesus rebuked false teachers who criticized Him, He also showed love and forgiveness in His forbearance, love, and sacrifice for them. Romans 12:14 and 17 remind us to bless those who persecute us and not repay evil for evil.

18. Read Luke 23:34. How did Jesus respond to His critics while on the cross suffering great agony?

19. Read Matthew 5:43–48. What did Jesus teach His followers about enemies?

Some People Are Critics of God, Not Us

While we are commanded to love and forgive our critics, it is also important to note that not all criticisms are valid. It is tempting to try to please critics. Romans 12 says, "If it is possible as far as it depends on you, live at peace with everyone." Examining Jesus' life shows that not all people can be pleased. Sometimes we need to depersonalize criticism and realize that it has nothing to do with us personally.

Paul labeled one group of critics as "enemies of the cross" (Philippians 3:18). John 15:18 says that the world sometimes hates us because it hated Jesus. Christians must be wary of critics who will analyze, criticize, misrepresent, and sometimes persecute every godly opinion or action. In a godless culture many critics feel compelled to criticize those who don't agree with their views. Maybe you wonder why it is so difficult to reason or talk with these critics. Perhaps it's because they cannot hear you. Their hard hearts have made them hard of hearing. Although this group of critics must be confronted with truth, they still need to see the compassion and love that Jesus offered His critics.

Lessons from Jesus' Dealings with Critics

- Critics will always find something to criticize, so don't take it personally.
- Not all criticism is valid, but it is valuable to analyze all criticism for helpful truth.
- Critics love to band together and can stir up contention.

- Critics need to be confronted about teaching error, even if the confrontation offends them.
- Critics are to be loved, prayed for, and forgiven.
- Enduring unjust criticism with patience can bring glory to God.

Studying Jesus' life helps us see how He dealt with critics. We see how He answered them, reasoned with them, corrected them, rebuked them, loved them, and died for them. It's not an easy example to follow, but because of the Spirit living within us, we can learn to deal with critics in a godly way.

Think about It

Consider these four questions this week as you think about your relationships:

1. Do I love my enemies with the same love I show my friends?
2. Do I pray for my critics as I pray for my friends?
3. Do I speak about my critics with the same respect as I do my friends?
4. Am I bold to speak truth to false teachers who lead people astray?

Action Steps

1. Identify one person who has criticized you.
2. Ask God to bless that person this week as if he or she was your best friend.
3. Do one tangible thing to show love and forgiveness to that person this week.

Verse

Memorize and think about Luke 6:35: "But love your enemies, do good, and lend, hoping for nothing in return; and your reward will be great, and you will be sons of the Most High. For He is kind to the unthankful and evil."

LESSON 6

How to Develop Compassion, Part 1

Sinners and Social Outcasts

"Therefore He is also able to save to the uttermost those who come to God through Him, since He always lives to make intercession for them" (Hebrews 7:25).

I WAS A PASTOR'S WIFE with four young children when national news began reporting on Jeffrey Dahmer, who killed and dismembered seventeen people and was accused of cannibalism. His crimes left the nation shocked and disgusted. But the story did not end there. While most of the nation stood back horrified, two individuals decided that Jeffrey Dahmer was worth redeeming. Apparently a church member in Virginia and a prison minister in Oklahoma both sent Dahmer Bible study materials.

"After studying the Bible in prison for a while," Dahmer said, "I have accepted [Jesus] as my Lord and Savior." Though no one can know if he was sincere, it's possible that one of the most twisted serial killers was saved. Interestingly, many people were furious that such a sinful person would be offered forgiveness, and some condemned the ones who showed him grace.

I realized that the response to him showcased three typical

responses to what we term "sinful people." First, some (like me) were horrified by the sin but did nothing. Second, many judged Dahmer unworthy of God's forgiveness. Third, a few reached out with a message of mercy, knowing that God can change anyone.

As we begin this study about sinners, consider which acts Christians typically categorize as "big sins." (Theologically we know there are no large and small sins, but be honest about which sins seem most offensive to you.) Then consider how you typically respond to the people who commit these sins (e.g., avoid, engage, criticize, complain about, love, include). As we examine Jesus' life, see how He responded to the sinful people He encountered.

Why It's Difficult to Embrace Radical Sinners

It's tempting for us Christians to restrict ourselves to church relationships to prevent sinful contamination. While this fortress mentality provides a buffer from the world's evil, it also can prevent our light and salt from permeating the soil of society. While trying to obey the command not to love the world, do we sometimes abandon the people in it?

Jesus' life was less like a moat keeping sinners out and more like a bridge providing access to Him through mercy and grace. In studying Jesus' life in the Gospels, we'll examine His response to sinners and help clarify our responsibility to people we might not want to associate with at all.

1. Perhaps the first thing to review is how, according to Romans 5:5–8, God treats all sinners. How has this truth impacted you personally?

Jesus' Relationship with Sinners and Outcasts

Jesus invited a "big sinner" into His inner circle

Read Matthew 9:9–13 and Mark 2:14–17.

Early in Jesus' public ministry, He encountered Matthew, also called Levi, who was known as a sinner because of his profession as a tax collector. This profession usually involved bribery and extortion, but also betrayal, since Jewish men worked for the Roman government to collect taxes.

2. How did Jesus respond to this man everyone else regarded as a sinner?

3. How did the religious leaders of the day respond to Jesus' actions?

4. Read Matthew 9:13. What can we learn about interacting with sinners?

From history we know that Matthew became a dedicated follower of Jesus. His Gospel recounts Jesus as king and highlights many fulfilled Old Testament prophecies. Interestingly, Matthew went from his sinful profession to being one of Jesus' closest friends.

Because religious Pharisees misunderstood God's rules about purity, they felt that getting close to sinners made them unclean, not to mention uncomfortable. They worried that one atypical action to help a beaten stranger or to comfort a wayward woman could jeopardize their "holier than others" position. Jesus had no such inhibitions. Jesus knew sinfulness doesn't rub off when you sit next to people or speak to them, so He never differentiated between a prostitute needing help or a Pharisee asking for direction. All were sinners—sinners whom He had come to seek and to save.

Jesus was compassionate toward and forgiving of sinful people

Read John 8:3–12.

5. What accusations did the Pharisees make against the woman?

6. How did Jesus encourage her accusers to focus on their own sin?

7. What was Jesus' admonition to the woman at the end of this encounter?

It is interesting that the one person who was truly without sin and could justifiably punish this woman is the one who displayed the most compassion and love toward her. Instead of a tongue-lashing for ignoring His clearly laid out Ten Commandments, Jesus showed mercy and grace. Yet He also did not make light of her sin and told her to sin no more.

Jesus sought sinful people

Read Luke 19:1–10.

8. How does this passage describe Zacchaeus and the effort it took for him to see Jesus?

9. What transformation happened to Zacchaeus?

10. How did the religious leaders respond to Jesus?

This is a familiar account because of a well-known children's song, but the account highlights Jesus' compassion for sinners. Amid the throng He looked up and saw Zacchaeus. Why would Jesus look past His many adoring followers and focus on someone in a tree? Jesus was simply doing what He came to do: search for the lost. It was no secret to Jesus that Zacchaeus was a tax collector, a big sinner. Yet Jesus made a special effort to reach out to him and spend time with him.

Read John 4:4–26.

This well-known Bible account is about another woman who had no doubts about her sinfulness. During her conversation with Jesus, He pointed out that she had had five husbands and was currently living in immorality. But some aspects of this account often get overlooked. The passage says Jesus needed to go through Samaria, which was unusual given the rift between the Jews and the Samaritans. Then He stopped at a well, although Jews were not supposed to eat or drink from the cups of sinful Samaritans.

11. Who initiated the conversation recorded in John 4:4–7?

12. According to John 4:27, how did Jesus' disciples respond to this impromptu meeting?

13. What, according to John 4:39–42, resulted from Jesus seeking this fallen woman?

It's doubtful that this woman would have attended a synagogue to hear Jesus. Her shame and regrets might have kept her from ever seeking Him at all. But He chose to engage her personally. Jesus' choice to speak to a woman and a Samaritan broke many cultural taboos, yet it was her conversion that caused many people to believe in Him. The disciples spent the day in town trying to avoid contamination, thus failing to touch anyone with their knowledge of Jesus. But this woman's dramatic transformation was obvious to those in her town, and it impacted them for eternity.

Jesus Recognized That Saved Sinners Are Great Witnesses

We should remember that often people with a difficult, sinful past can be the best evangelists. Several of my friends, including some pastors' wives, were once mired in sinful lifestyles and activities. But when someone shared the truth of the gospel with them, God transformed them, and they now share the powerful testimony of His redeeming grace. This was true for Zacchaeus and the unnamed woman at the well, but also for the demon-possessed man in Gadarenes. In this account Jesus sought a man who was a sinner and social outcast.

Read Luke 8:26–39.

14. Describe the man who was demon possessed.

15. In verse 39, after Jesus delivered this man from his demons, what did Jesus ask the man to do?

Jesus Was Not Ashamed to Be Seen with Great Sinners

Read Luke 7:36–39.

This account highlights several important facts about Jesus' dealings with sinners. Since Jesus was quite popular, it was an honor for Simon to have Jesus eat at his house. But this Pharisee seemed to think he was worthy of the honor. Imagine how upset he must have been when a sinful woman burst in, began washing Jesus' feet, and poured precious perfume on them. The passage does not explain whether it was her clothes or her reputation that gave away this woman's sinful lifestyle, but it was apparently no secret.

16. How did Simon respond to this woman's actions?

Read Luke 7:40–48.

Simon was right that as a prophet (and even the God-Man), Jesus knew exactly what type of woman was touching Him, but Simon mistakenly assumed he knew how Jesus would treat sinners. Simon decided that this woman was not worthy to be in his home or to be near Jesus.

17. Reread verses 40–43. What was the point of the story Jesus told about the two debtors?

18. Why was this woman eager to serve and love Jesus, while the religious Pharisee ignored Jesus' needs upon entering his house?

Before Jesus' birth, the angel declared, "You shall call His name Jesus, for He will save His people from their sins" (Matthew 1:21). This was His mission. So, when faced with a woman many counted unworthy, Jesus said, "Your sins are forgiven" (Luke 7:48). She might have been the least likely candidate in the room, but she was the one to whom Jesus granted forgiveness. Simon learned a lesson that day: God's big arms of forgiveness embrace every person, every style, and certainly every sin.

But Simon made another, more serious mistake while slapping the woman with a "sinner" label. He forgot that under his self-righteous robes, his heart was branded with that same label. Simon might not have looked or acted like a sinner. He was probably a very religious, well-groomed, highly respected, and well-educated sinner, but he was still a sinner according to Romans 3:23. Godliness comes from God's sanctification, not from a list of rules. Simon needed Jesus' mercy and forgiveness just as much as the woman did.

Even if we understand that we are also sinners, we have a desire to maintain a "them and us" mentality when it comes to "big sinners" like prostitutes, terrorists, homosexuals, murderers, and the like. Usually those who are that sinful appear on our prayer lists much more frequently than at our dinner table. We want God to win them and change them so they will fit in with our lifestyle, not thinking that they need someone who cares enough to respond compassionately to their lifestyle.

The account of the sinful woman who washed Jesus' feet shows that it is easy to forget our own sinfulness and lack of merit before God.

> "He saved us, not because of righteous things we had done, but because of his mercy." (Titus 3:5, NIV)

After studying how Jesus interacted with overtly sinful people, it becomes apparent that He truly loved sinners. He knew their past, present, and future sins; and while they were depraved, He loved them and died for them (Romans 5:8).

When we are disgusted by the ugly nature of someone's sin, consider a holy God becoming a human and living among people whose sins were all as filthy rags. Consider how the God-Man, Who knew no sin, responded to these sinners.

First, Jesus' mission was to seek and to save those who are lost, and every human obviously falls into that category. Romans 5:8 declares that while we were yet sinners, Christ died for us.

Second, Jesus wasn't fooled by pious exteriors, well-dressed liars, or outwardly spiritual personas. Some people do the right things, say the right words, and never go near the wrong places. But Jesus sees the heart and mind and knows "all have sinned, and come short of the glory of God" (Romans 3:23, KJV) because "there is none righteous, no, not one" (Romans 3:10). All sinners look the same to Him, so He loves and forgives them all with the same love and mercy.

Third, Jesus knew that those who recognized their sinfulness accepted His forgiveness more readily than those who thought their high moral standard would buy acceptance with God. Those He forgave much, loved Him that much more. He made a great effort to connect with those burdened down with sin and shame.

19. Record the descriptions of unsaved people given in Titus 3:3–5.

How easy it is to forget the depth from which God rescued us. This attitude happens if we begin to judge sins on a human scale: the abortionist is worse than the gossip; the murderer is more sinful than the jealous; the prostitute is far worse than the proud religious man. But the Bible puts everyone in the same category when it comes to sin. If you read a list of sins, such as in Galatians 5:19–21, you will read some huge sins—like sorcery, adultery, and murder—listed right next to selfish ambition, jealousy, and envy. Some of those sins we would never do, but others we might be guilty of regularly. God is holy, and all sin is offensive to Him, so each of us is just as much a great sinner as any other person.

> "For whoever keeps the whole law and yet stumbles at just one point is guilty of breaking all of it." (James 2:10)

Think about It

Here are Bible verses and two questions to ponder this week as you think about your relationships:

1. Write out Titus 3:4–7 below, personalizing this passage with the words "me" and "I."

2. Write a list of infamous people known for inhumane crimes against humanity. Next to it, write a list of the most noble, caring, loving people who have lived sacrificial lives. Which of these groups needed Jesus' mercy, washing of regeneration, and renewing of the Holy Spirit? Which of these do we usually seek out?

Action Steps

1. Do you have "big sinners" in your sphere of influence? In your family or workplace or neighborhood? Write their names on your prayer list, not simply for their salvation but for God to give you a true heart of love for them and to provide a way for you to reach out to them as Jesus would. Perhaps you could also invite them to dinner.
2. Reject seclusion from the world and submersion in the world. But accept inclusion of people into your world. Invite them to see what God did for a big sinner like you.
3. Consider volunteering at a ministry that reaches out to these people, such as jails, pregnancy resource centers, and halfway houses.

Verse

Memorize and think about Hebrews 7:25: "Therefore He is also able to save to the uttermost those who come to God through Him, since He always lives to make intercession for them."

LESSON 7

How to Develop Compassion, Part 2

The Poor, Sick, and Needy

"Therefore I command you, saying, 'You shall open your hand wide to your brother, to your poor and your needy, in your land'" (Deuteronomy 15:11).

MOST OF US ARE AWARE of the pain and suffering in the world. Social media and news agencies have brought world hunger, human trafficking, homeless orphans, and other needy people onto our televisions and into our consciousness. As Christians we are grieved over those situations and have pity on those less fortunate than ourselves. But this pity does not always translate into action. Why? Are we so far removed from the suffering that it's easier to ignore it than fight against it? Is it too upsetting to stop and consider the desperate plight of people? Could it be that because the needs are so great, we feel helpless and don't know where to start?

It could be all the above, but it also could be that we have never looked closely at how important compassion is to our Lord. By studying Jesus' heart in the Gospels, we will see how His heart of compassion compelled Him to action. In the book *Awake*, the author reminds us that "compassion is not pity. It is not feeling sorry for someone. . . . True compassion—the compassion that Jesus had in the Bible when he was 'moved with compassion'—is more than awareness and a wish. This kind of compassion requires movement, advocacy and action. Pity sees and even feels, but compassion touches the need."[1]

You cannot read far in the Gospels without realizing that Jesus not only said He had compassion for people, but He personally reached out and made a difference in their lives.

A Compassionate Healer

The disciples had learned of the horrible beheading of John the Baptist. They buried his body and came to tell Jesus, Who decided to withdraw from the crowds by boat to a desolate place.

1. Read Matthew 14:13–14.
   (a) Why did Jesus leave for a deserted place?

   (b) How did Jesus respond to the people who followed Him during this difficult time?

2. Read Matthew 4:23–25. Record what Jesus did as He traveled throughout Galilee.

3. In Matthew 8:5–13 how did Jesus show compassion to the centurion, who was Roman?

   Read Luke 5:12–15

4. According to Luke 5:12, what need brought a man to see Jesus?

5. Compare how Jesus healed the centurion's servant with the way He healed the leper in Luke 5:13.

This event must have had a significant impact on Jesus' disciples, since it is mentioned in three of the four Gospels. Lepers with their contagious disease and disfigured bodies were to be avoided, not touched. Even the disciples must have wondered why Jesus would touch an infected man. But Mark's account of this event mentions Jesus being moved with compassion. For the leper who had been ostracized, condemned to live alone outside society, Jesus' touch might have meant as much as his healing. Again, Jesus' love for people caused Him to intervene in their lives in practical ways as well as spiritual ways.

6. Read the following verses. What caused Jesus to have compassion in these encounters, and how did He respond to the needs?

   Matthew 15:32

   Matthew 20:30–34

   Mark 2:5–12

   Luke 7:11–13

Jesus Met Physical Needs to Address Real Needs

It is easy to look at these and many other Bible passages and see only the miracles Jesus did, which are impossible for us. We can't heal the paralyzed, cure the demon possessed, feed thousands, or heal all types of diseases. But perhaps we gloss over the bigger picture of what we can do. When Jesus encountered needy people, He didn't turn away from their suffering; He responded to their needs. His relationship with the needy was often based on noticing them, recognizing their physical or temporal needs, but ultimately drawing attention to their spiritual needs.

Read John 4:46–53.

7. Why did the nobleman, or royal official, seek Jesus?

8. What was the result of the encounter with Jesus?

9. Read the following passages. What do they say about God's compassion for the needy?

   Psalm 113:4–7

   Proverbs 31:8–9

10. What challenge to believers is given in 1 John 3:16–17?

Christians have corporately established agencies such as rescue missions to help the homeless, soup kitchens to feed the poor, or clothes closets to clothe the needy. I've worked at several pregnancy resource centers, which offer hope and help to women struggling with unplanned pregnancies. Each of these agencies offers practical solutions to the needy and shows compassionate care along with the life-giving message of the gospel. Involvement in these agencies is a wonderful way to meet the needs beyond our reach. But Jesus assumed His followers would be personally involved. In the beatitudes He mentions several times, "when you give to the needy," not if you give. Perhaps we believe that having these agencies absolves us of our responsibility to personally be involved with needy people who cross our paths.

Read Luke 10:25–37.

11. What two commands are mentioned as important in the Law (v. 27)?

12. Who were the principal characters in the story of the Good Samaritan?

13. Why would the Samaritan be the least likely person to stop and help this man?

14. In what way was the Samaritan personally inconvenienced to help this stranger?

Perhaps the biggest reason we hesitate to get involved in the lives of the poor and needy is fear of what it will cost. Time? Money? Inconvenience? Maybe all the above?

Unlike Luke 10:25–37, Matthew 19 recounts Jesus' encounter with a rich young man who showed signs of greed and selfishness. Most people don't identify with this man, because they certainly don't feel rich; but according to world stats, anyone with clean water to drink, adequate food to eat, safe housing, and access to health care is wealthy. In fact, the Global Wealth List says, "An income of $32,400 per year would allow someone to be among the top 1% of income earners in the world."[2]

15. In Matthew 19:21 what did Jesus ask the man to do as a sign of his commitment to Jesus?

16. Read Matthew 19:22–24. What was the outcome of the encounter?

When confronted with giving up what he considered "his" belongings to give to the poor, this man decided the price was too high. This scenario makes me rather uncomfortable. I've never been asked to give up all "my" belongings, and I wonder how I would respond if I was. Although theoretically and theologically I understand that everything I have is God's, practically speaking it is tough to imagine giving it all over to the poor to follow Jesus. So, like the rich young ruler, we need to beware lest the lure of consumerism draws us away from giving and into the trap of materialism that God warns against.

I learned recently of an American family whose father got called out of town suddenly. He gave his eldest child money to care for the whole family. While the dad was gone, the eldest bought himself a home and some nice furnishings. But as expenses poured in, less money was available to share with other family members. Eventually the eldest lived luxuriously while the rest of the family lived in poverty. Of course, he occasionally felt pity on them and sent a few dollars to help, but since the money had been given to him to manage, he felt justified in keeping tight control of it.

It seems so outrageous to us. How could this man neglect caring for his brothers and sisters, especially when the money was given by their father? Yet the story I heard was about many of us. We are that older brother who has hoarded resources given to us by our Heavenly Father that were meant to be shared with our brothers and sisters around the world. Luke 12:48 says, "From everyone who has been given much, much will be demanded; and from the one who has been entrusted with much, much more will be asked" (NIV).

A Reason for Hope

At the root of many social problems lies not just lack of money or support, but hopelessness. People who are hungry or homeless or trafficked or in any crisis can feel that no one cares for them and that things will never change. Loving people as Jesus did means caring about their struggles. When even one person who cares about their needs, hurts, and burdens steps into their situation, it can give them hope. And then that person can point them to the One Who gives hope.

17. Read Ephesians 2:12–13. Why are people ultimately without hope in the world?

18. Read 1 Peter 3:15. What does God ask of believers, who have hope?

    Read Ephesians 2:4–8.

19. What words are used in this text to highlight God's compassion to the world?

20. What is the ultimate answer of hope that every person needs?

Just as we take our wealth and possessions for granted, we often take for granted the joy and security we experience because we know Jesus Christ personally. As we share our earthly possessions with others, we need to be ready to not only show God's love but also to give an answer of the hope that is in us. The intersection of needy people with our lives could be the only opportunity they have to hear the life-changing message of the gospel.

Jesus' compassion is evident in each relationship throughout Scripture. That we can't perform miraculous deeds like He did does not mean we cannot develop His eyes of compassion for the sick, hurting, and needy people around us. Having His compassion involves opening our eyes to the plight of the people that God puts in our path and being willing to do something about their need. As Paul reminded Timothy in 1 Timothy 6:17–18, "Command those who are rich in this present world not to be arrogant nor to put their hope in wealth. . . . Command them to do good, to be rich in good deeds, and to be generous and willing to share" (NIV). If it takes money, time, and effort, we must recognize that everything God has given us is a stewardship from Him to care for the needs around us.

Think about It

1. Do we ever shirk personal responsibility with those God places in our path and assume someone else or some agency will care for them?
2. How can we as individuals show mercy, kindness, and love to the needy?
3. What prevents us from getting involved with them?

Action Steps

1. Make a list of all types of needy people.
2. Pray that God will open your eyes to have His compassion for those around you.
3. Look people in the eyes, engage in conversation, and do not rush past those God puts in your path. Try to give them one word of encouragement and hope.

Verse

Memorize and think about Deuteronomy 15:11: "Therefore I command you, saying, 'You shall open your hand wide to your brother, to your poor and your needy, in your land.'"

Endnotes

[1]Noel Brewer Yeatts, *Awake: Doing a World of Good One Person at a Time* (Ada, MI: Baker Books, 2012), 73.

[2]Daniel Kurt, "Are You in the World's Top 1 Percent?" *Investopedia* (Sept. 25, 2019), https://www.investopedia.com/articles/personal-finance/050615/are-you-top-one-percent-world.asp.

LESSON 8

Don't Play to the Crowds

"But when He saw the multitudes, He was moved with compassion for them, because they were weary and scattered, like sheep having no shepherd" (Matthew 9:36).

SOON AFTER JESUS BEGAN His public ministry, His popularity soared, and crowds of people followed Him. Some might deduce this was a sign of His effective ministry, since increased numbers is often the goal of events. Whether individuals are hosting a fundraiser, a concert, or a church event, most planners try to do some advertising to increase their attendance. I recently saw some tips on how to draw a crowd, which listed things like setting goals, advertising with eye-catching ads, promoting in advance, and marketing events to a wide group of people. But it was the summary statement that caught my attention: the key to a successful event is strong attendance. Without a supportive crowd, your event could fall flat.

This might be true in business, but what about in Christian ministries or events? It's tempting to judge success solely on the size of the crowd, but a study of how Jesus dealt with crowds seems to indicate that numbers don't always indicate impact. As we continue to study Christ and His relationships, it is important to observe how Jesus responded to and interacted with the multitude who chose to follow Him.

1. Read Matthew 4:23–25.
   (a) Name some things Jesus did throughout Galilee.

   (b) Which of these do you think caused crowds to follow Him?

The ability to draw a large crowd is not unique to Jesus. Professional athletes draw crowds because of their athletic skills. Television personalities draw crowds because of name recognition and glamor. Political leaders draw crowds because of their influence. Even Christian speakers draw large crowds for their great preaching and Bible teaching. But Jesus' interaction and treatment of the crowds seems unique. Let's follow Jesus through the pages of the Gospels to see His response to the multitudes that followed Him.

2. Read Matthew 14:14. How did Jesus' response to the crowd differ from most celebrities today who observe fans gathered for an event?

3. Read Mark 3:7–10. Look at a map of Israel during Jesus' time. Where did all these people come from to follow Jesus?

Jesus Never Sought Crowds

Although popularity is measured in numbers, heart change is measured individually. Perhaps Jesus' view of successful ministry can be seen by His response to two blind beggars who diverted His attention from the crowd. In Matthew 20 the crowd rebuked the men who were calling for Jesus and told them to be quiet, but Jesus had compassion on them and stopped to heal them. He ignored the crowd to focus on individuals.

Read Mark 2:1–12.

4. How did Jesus' popularity spread?

5. What was the first thing Jesus did in this gathering?

6. How was the healing of the paralyzed man used to further the gospel?

Although crowds were watching, Jesus did not heal to please the crowds or to show off His power. He sought to please only His Father.

> "And truly Jesus did many other signs in the presence of His disciples, which are not written in this book; but these are written that you may believe that Jesus is the Christ, the Son of God, and that believing you may have life in His name." (John 20:30–31)

Jesus' purpose for healing didn't waiver, no matter what crowds thought or said. He wasn't interested in drawing a crowd, but in impacting individuals with the gospel. His miracles were signs to verify His claim to deity and help people believe.

Jesus Sought Solitude Away from Crowds

Jesus often retreated from large crowds. Matthew 8:18 states that "when Jesus saw the crowd around him, he gave orders to cross to the other side" (NIV). Mark 1 relates that crowds constantly sought Jesus. Early in the morning He went to pray. One day the disciples came to Him, saying, "Everyone is looking for you." Jesus replied, "Let us go somewhere else . . . so I can preach there also. That is why I have come" (v. 38). Jesus' goal was to seek and to save the lost, and He did not allow crowds to dictate His schedule or ministry.

Crowds followed Him, but He never followed the crowd.

Crowds were enamored with Him, but He wasn't enamored with them.

Crowds listened to Him, but He never listened to the crowd.

Jesus Knew the Dangers of Crowds

Although people followed Jesus wherever He went, instead of seeking them, He was skeptical of them and identified some dangers of crowds.

Crowds want something

After Thanksgiving, throngs of Americans seeking special deals fill stores, malls, and parking lots. These Black Friday crowds have literally caused stampedes and brawls at stores. Why? Because people gather to get something they want. Whether they are shopping for a toy or a television, they can grow angry when they don't get it.

Crowds were the same in Jesus' day. People expected something and became violent when disappointed. Early in His ministry while Jesus was in Jerusalem, many people believed in His name because they saw His miracles. John 2:24 says, "But Jesus did not commit Himself to them, because He knew all men." Jesus reacted differently to crowds because He understood the crowd mentality and fickleness.

Read Luke 4:14–30.

7. How did the people initially respond to Jesus (vv. 14–15, 20, 22)?

8. What angered the crowd, and how did the people respond (vv. 23–30)?

9. How does this incident reveal the crowd's real goal regarding following Jesus?

In Matthew 11 Jesus addressed the crowds that had thronged around John the Baptist. Jesus asked them why they had followed John to the wilderness but refused to listen to his message of repentance. "Then He began to rebuke the cities in which most of His mighty works had been done, because they did not repent" (Matthew 11:20). It's obvious that Jesus was not interested in numbers of followers; He was interested in people's repentance and obedience.

Crowds can be swayed easily

Read Matthew 21:8–11.

Crowds can be dangerous in another sense also. Sometimes in a large group, it's tempting to listen to the crowd, go with the flow, and be swayed by the loudest voice. During the triumphal entry in Matthew 21, everyone was crying hosanna and blessing Jesus' name. It was easy to join in. But not many days later the same crowds shouted to crucify Him. When things looked bad, they turned on Jesus because the thrill was gone and they had never been committed to Him.

10. How did the crowds respond when asked about Jesus' fate (Matthew 27:20–23)?

Read John 6:35–66.

John 6 highlights how easily a crowd can vacillate, or waver. After Jesus fed the five thousand, crowds sought to make Jesus their king. They said, "This is truly the Prophet who is to come into the world." When Jesus "perceived that they were about to come and take Him by force to make Him king, He departed again to the mountain by Himself alone" (vv. 14–15). The next day when they found Him, He told them they did not seek Him for food that endures to eternal life, but for a full stomach.

11. List some things Jesus taught about Himself in John 6:35–40.

12. How did the crowd respond to this teaching in verses 41–42?

13. What did Jesus teach them in verses 46–51?

14. What caused their initial misunderstanding in verse 52?

15. What happened to many of the crowd of so-called disciples in verses 60 and 66?

Instead of seeking clarification or staying to hear all that Jesus was teaching, many people simply left. Jesus taught a hard message that was difficult to grasp. In a crowd of uncommitted people it was easier to just walk away. But if they had listened to Jesus' message that He was the One necessary for eternal life, they might have been willing to stay. As Peter declares in John 6:68, there is no one else that can give eternal life.

People can easily join a crowd without making a commitment to anything except experiencing the moment itself. But crowds who follow with no commitment often scatter when pressure or difficulty comes. Since crowds usually seek the easy path, not the narrow road, they are often wrong and lead people astray (Matthew 7:13–15).

Jesus did not want large groups of uncommitted people. Instead He wanted men and women to commit their lives to Him, to follow Him personally, and to believe in Him even when things looked difficult. He knew His followers would eventually pay a price for their belief in Him, so their faith needed to be real.

People in the Crowd Had Divided Opinions of Jesus

Scripture makes it clear that Jesus spoke truth that was sometimes controversial, and His listeners had divided opinions of Him. Some came to find fault in Him, while others came to hear His message. In fact, many times throughout Scripture when Jesus preached or performed miracles, the crowd would be split in its response.

16. In John 7:12–20 the crowd listening to Jesus was confused about His identity. List the various responses of people listening to Him.

Sometimes it's hard to find clarity about personal beliefs in large groups. Knowing the crowd couldn't handle the truth, Jesus often took His disciples aside to give more in-depth teaching.

Crowds Can Be a Great Tool to Spread the Gospel

Jesus did not, however, always dispel crowds, because sometimes crowds were an opportunity to teach multitudes of people at one time. Matthew 5:1–2 says, "And seeing the multitudes, He went up on a mountain, and when He was seated His disciples came to Him. Then He opened His mouth and taught them." The mountainside acoustics allowed Jesus to share His sermon with a multitude. Matthew 7:28–29 says, "And so it was, when Jesus had ended these sayings, that the people were astonished at His teaching, for He taught them as one having authority, and not as the scribes." It is interesting to note that their response was not necessarily belief, but amazement.

In Mark 4 Jesus again taught a huge multitude, but this time from a boat in the sea.

17. Read Mark 4:1–9, 13–20. What does the parable of the sower and the seed explain about sowing the Word?

18. According to Mark 4:33–34, what was unique about Jesus' time with His disciples after the crowds were gone?

I love going to large conferences. It's exhilarating to sing with thousands of voices and share a great experience. But in a large crowd, it's hard to really hear. Distractions are everywhere. Your mind can wander, and it's easy to tune out even outstanding speakers. Jesus knew that people in the crowd were hearing His voice but not necessarily listening to the truth He was sharing, so He presented general truths. Later He explained His statements to His true followers.

Once we realize that the size of the crowd seemed insignificant to Jesus, perhaps that fact will free us from undue pressure to play to the crowds and will keep us focused on the effective ministry of making disciples one by one. From Jesus' ministry we can conclude that the effectiveness of ministry can be seen, not by how many people gather to hear, but by how many people believe, obey, and produce fruit as true followers of Jesus.

We have been conditioned to believe that large crowds are the mark of effective ministry, but after surveying Jesus' life, it might be well to draw some important conclusions about crowds.

Lessons We Can Learn from Observing Jesus and Crowds

- Our purpose should be making disciples, not drawing crowds.
- We should make sure to follow God's pattern for ministry and not pattern ministry to draw crowds. Crowds should never dictate our ministry.
- Crowds can be exciting and fun but also dangerous and manipulative.
- It's wonderful when crowds gather to hear the truth, but we cannot assume everyone will understand or agree.
- Although crowds are a great way to initiate contact, personal interaction with individuals in crowds is the best way to make disciples.
- Faith in God must be personal, not corporate, and it needs to be firm enough to stand against the whims of the crowd.
- We should have compassion on the throngs of people who don't know Jesus and have no shepherd or Savior.

Think about It

Consider these two questions this week as you work on your relationships:

1. In which setting have you been most impacted for Christ: a large crowd, a small group, or one-on-one?
2. Are you disappointed when a smaller group attends your event instead of being excited that you have more personal interaction?

Action Steps

1. Look for one person who might be interested in further discipleship from your church and try to connect.
2. List opportunities you have to impact people in a small group that are not available in a large crowd.

Verse

Memorize and think about Matthew 9:36: "But when He saw the multitudes, He was moved with compassion for them, because they were weary and scattered, like sheep having no shepherd."

LESSON 9

Jesus' Relationship with the Father

"For I have come down from heaven, not to do My own will, but the will of Him who sent Me" (John 6:38).

IN PREVIOUS LESSONS we studied Jesus' ability to engage various groups of people. He had close friends, sought outcasts and sinners, dealt with His critics, cared for His family, and stopped to minister to individuals. As we conclude the study of relationships based on Jesus' life, it is easy to be overwhelmed. Too many people with too many needs come to mind. How can we ever decide who needs our time most? How do we set priorities for connecting with those who need to hear the gospel? When Jesus came to earth, He faced a world full of needy people. He never met a person who did not legitimately need Him. Yet He never hurried. He never seemed overwhelmed. He was not confused about His mission. How was that possible? We might say it is because He is God in the flesh. But the strategy implemented by Jesus is available to all believers. The Gospels reveal that Jesus' relationship with the Father was the key to everything Jesus accomplished on earth. This is the relationship God has invited all of us to have with Him.

Jesus Relied on the Father's Direction

According to Matthew 9, when Jesus visited nearby cities and villages, He saw a world full of people with serious physical problems and even more serious spiritual problems. His heart of compassion went out to them. Although He healed many people of sickness and disease, He did not heal every person on earth. He did not right every wrong. In fact, not everyone who met Jesus had his or her sins forgiven. Have you ever wondered how Jesus determined to whom He would minister?

1. Read Matthew 9:36–38. What did Jesus tell the disciples to do in response to the many needs that were in the world?

Note that the Gospels don't record Jesus rushing around trying to meet all the needs of all the people Himself. Neither did He guilt the disciples into personally tackling this plentiful harvest. Instead, Jesus specifically directed them to pray and ask God to send someone. Seeking God's intervention acknowledges that God alone knows the needs, that people can best meet those needs, and that participating in prayer is important. This pattern is not always what comes to our minds when we see a need. Typically, my thought process goes something like this:

I notice a need. No one else is meeting that need, so I determine I must try to meet that need myself (even if I'm overcommitted, ignoring my own responsibilities, or unable to offer a good solution).

That do-it-yourself model seems noble, but it does not take into consideration that without God's help we are powerless. (Some people ignore the need altogether, which is not God's plan either.) Jesus said the process is to go to God in prayer and ask Him to send just the right person into the harvest. During prayer God might prompt us to go personally, but then we are acting out of obedience instead of misguided guilt. Jesus took the approach of seeking His Father's direction in every situation.

2. According to Mark 1:35–38, how did Jesus respond to His disciples when they told Him everyone was looking for Him?

3. In John 6:38 what did Jesus say was His mission?

4. Read Luke 22:39–44. How does Jesus' prayer on the Mount of Olives showcase that doing the Father's will was not always easy?

5. According to Philippians 2:6–8, how did Jesus demonstrate obedience to the Father?

These key passages show how Jesus determined His course of action on earth. When Jesus acted, it was under the Father's direction and will. Perhaps you are thinking, "I would love to follow God's will if I only knew what it was."

6. What special resources did Jesus give to those who would carry on His work after He returned to Heaven?

   John 15:14–15

   John 16:13–14

   John 17:8–9

How easy it is to get up in the morning, plan your day, maybe look at a passage of Scripture, but forget to consult God for direction. We usually take time to sync our planner or calendar with our family, but we do not always stop to submit it to God's Word or pray about each detail. Jesus took time to spend with His Father despite a crowded, almost impossible schedule. He knew that this practice would not only help Him be productive but would also put His priorities in line with His Father's.

7. What practical actions can we take to allow God to dictate our schedule and priorities?

Jesus Relied on His Father's Power

8. What was the key to Jesus' power on earth, according to John 5:19?

We sometimes look at Jesus' earthly ministry and see only His divine side. We forget that according to Philippians 2:7, He "emptied himself, by taking the form of a servant, being born in the likeness of men" (ESV). On earth, Jesus lay aside His independent powers and subjected Himself to the Father in all that He accomplished.

Ironically, while Jesus the God-Man was dependent on His Father for strength, we often act self-sufficient. However, when we tackle relationship issues in our own strength—whether conflict, connecting with people, or sharing the gospel—we usually end up exhausted, burned out, and ineffective. Learning from Jesus' dependence should teach us to remember from Whom we will receive power.

9. According to Philippians 4:13, from where did Paul get the strength to endure his difficult ministry life?

10. What did Paul say in Romans 1:16–17 about sharing the gospel with others?

11. Read John 15:5.

    (a) What can you learn from John 15:5 about relying on God?

    (b) How does John 15:5 compare to Jesus' reliance in John 5:30?

Whether ministering to people around us who have needs or sharing the gospel, we need to know where we get power. We must depend on God, not self. When it comes to the gospel, we are not the power. The gospel is the power of God to salvation; we are simply the conduits. Although a hose has no power of its own, it can spread life-giving water from another source. Our lives can spread the life-giving gospel, but sometimes we are like a clogged hose—so filled with ourselves that the power of the gospel cannot be released.

Jesus Sought His Father's Approval

In every deed Jesus did on earth, His priority was to please God. At Jesus' baptism (Matthew 3:17) God declared audibly from Heaven, "This is My beloved Son, in whom I am well pleased." God's words were repeated on a mountain with three disciples as witnesses (Matthew 17:5). Regardless of what challenge Jesus faced, He knew that one relationship was more important than all others. Whether tempted or tried or beaten or scorned, Jesus sought God's approval over all others.

12. In Matthew 22:36–38 what did Jesus say is the greatest commandment?

13. Read John 5:38–40. Although studying the Scripture is important, what is essential in knowing and loving God?

14. Read John 5:41–44. Why is it dangerous to seek approval from people?

15. Fill in the blanks from John 8:28–29 (NKJV).

    "Then Jesus said to them, 'When you lift up the Son of Man, then you will know that I am He, and that ________ ____; but as My Father taught Me, I speak these things. And He who sent Me is with Me. The Father has not left Me alone, for ____ ____.'"

That Jesus tried to please and serve God alone is significant. This is a defining factor in the study of relationships, because when we serve God, we might find a time when no one except God is pleased with us. Jeremiah faced this, Stephen faced this, and certainly Jesus faced it. Ministering to people to please God is not the same as ministering to people to please them. Paul bluntly told the Thessalonians that he had come to please God, not them. (You might even beware of times when you are pleasing everyone around you but when God is not pleased.) Seeking God's will does not mean that everyone's needs will be met or that everyone will be happy with you. But it means you are focused on pleasing God alone.

Jesus Finished His Work

At the end of His life, Jesus made an amazing statement. He had finished the work God had for Him. Many people were still lost. Many were suffering with disease or hunger or abuse. How could Jesus make this statement?

16. What statement in John 17:4 explains why Jesus could say with confidence that He had finished His work?

17. In Acts 20:24 what was Paul's desire concerning His ministry?

18. What steps can help you determine your priorities and your daily plan for relationships so that you can finish the task God has for you to do?

Every relationship takes a portion of our time and energy. Therefore, it's natural to feel overwhelmed by the needs of people and frustrated by our lack of time to minister to them effectively. But the answer from God's Word and exemplified in Jesus' life is to seek God's direction and strength to prioritize our relationships and maximize our impact for Christ. This allows us to be obedient to God yet avoid the trap of overcommitment and discouragement.

For you, this might mean dropping some relationships that God has not given you or seeking new relationships with individuals you have ignored in the past. It might mean reprioritizing the relationships you currently have in order to fulfill the duties only you can fulfill. But whatever God gives you to do, He'll provide power for you to finish the task.

Think about It

Ponder these questions as you think about your relationships this week:

1. When have you taken on too many people's needs without asking God for direction first?
2. Did you feel obligated?
3. Did you try to please others?
4. How did it turn out?

Action Step

1. Commit to daily asking God to control your to-do list.
2. Be open to interruptions, new relationships, and new priorities that God places in your daily path.

Verse

Memorize and think about John 6:38: "For I have come down from heaven, not to do My own will, but the will of Him who sent Me."

Summary

"He who says he abides in Him ought himself also to walk just as He walked" (1 John 2:6).

Principles to Help Us Engage like Jesus

1. Prioritize your relationship with God above all. Draw near to God, like a deer pants for water. A relationship with Him is the only one we cannot live without. Knowing Him will clarify all other relationships.
2. Seek God's strength and wisdom. Never attempt the smallest task without God. If the task is from Him, He will provide strength.
3. Set godly priorities from God's Word. Make sure your priorities line up with the principles in the Bible: God, family, others.
4. Show God's compassion for sinners and outcasts. Seek people who might be afraid or ashamed to explore spiritual matters. Shower them with the same love and mercy you have received from the Lord.
5. Be generous to the needy. God has entrusted you with material blessings, talents, abilities, and more. Seek ways to share these blessings to bless others.
6. Seek to minister to people effectively—whether in large crowds or small settings. Disciple the people around you and never worry about numbers.
7. Show mercy and forgiveness to those who hurt you. Allow God to correct any wrongs against you, and seek to live at peace with others.

8. Place a high priority and value on your family. God values family highly and has given you a special role that cannot be duplicated. Love and serve your family well.
9. Seek God's approval, not man's. Listen to God. Do what He says. Seek His approval. Never worry if you are not thanked, appreciated, or honored. You need to please only Him.

Leader's Guide

Suggestions for Leaders

The effectiveness of a group Bible study usually depends on the leader and the women's commitment to prepare beforehand and interact during the study. You cannot totally control the second factor, but you have total control over the first one. These brief suggestions will help you be an effective Bible study leader.

Prepare each lesson a week in advance. During the week, read supplemental material and look for illustrations in the everyday events of your life and in the lives of others.

Encourage the women to complete each lesson before the meeting itself. This preparation will make the discussion more interesting.

The physical setting in which you meet will have some bearing on the study itself. Choose an informal setting that will encourage women to relax and participate. In addition to an informal setting, create an atmosphere in which women feel free to participate and be themselves.

During the discussion time, here are a few things to observe.

- Don't do all the talking. This study is not designed to be a lecture.
- Encourage discussion of each question by adding ideas and questions.
- Don't discuss controversial issues that will divide the group. (Differences of opinion are healthy; divisions are not.)
- Don't allow one woman to dominate the discussion. Use statements such as these to draw others into the study: "Let's hear from someone on this side of the room" (the side opposite the dominant talker); "Let's hear from someone who has not shared yet today."
- Stay on the subject. The tendency toward tangents is always possible in a discussion. One of your responsibilities as the leader is to keep the group on track.
- Don't get bogged down on a question that interests only one person.
- When there is no right or wrong answer to a question, the answer key says, "Personal answers." This doesn't mean that the question cannot be answered aloud, just that the question will be answered from a personal perspective. Feel free to invite women to respond aloud if they desire. But keep in mind the points listed above to keep your discussion uplifting and on track.

You may want to use the last fifteen minutes of the scheduled time for prayer. If you have a large group of learners, divide into smaller groups for prayer.

If you have a morning Bible study, encourage the women to go out for lunch with someone else from time to time. This is a good way to get acquainted. Occasionally you could plan a time when the women bring their own lunches or salads to share and eat together. These things help promote fellowship and friendship in the group.

The formats that follow are suggestions only. You can plan your own format, use one of these, or adapt one of these to your needs.

2-hour Bible Study

10:00—10:15	Coffee and fellowship time
10:15—10:30	Get-acquainted time *Have two women take five minutes each to tell something about themselves and their families.* *Also use this time to make announcements and, if appropriate, take an offering for the babysitters.*
10:30—11:45	Bible study *Leader guides discussion of the questions in the day's lesson.*
11:45—12:00	Prayer time

2-hour Bible Study

10:00—10:45	Bible lesson *Leader teaches a lesson on the content of the material. No discussion during this time.*
10:45—11:00	Coffee and fellowship
11:00—11:45	Discussion time *Divide into small groups with an appointed leader for each group. Discuss the questions in the day's lesson.*
11:45—12:00	Prayer time

1½-hour Bible Study

10:00—10:30	Bible study *Leader guides discussion of half the questions in the day's lesson.*
10:30—10:45	Coffee and fellowship
10:45—11:15	Bible study *Leader continues discussion of the questions in the day's lesson.*
11:15—11:30	Prayer time

Answers

Additional comments and explanations, where given, appear in parentheses after the answers.

LESSON 1

1. *Matt. 4:18–20, Simon and Andrew*—Jesus sought them while they fished near the Sea of Galilee; they followed Him. *Mark 10:17–22, a rich young ruler*—Jesus connected with him on the road when he asked Jesus a question, and He loved him; the man rejected Jesus. *Luke 7:2–6, a Roman centurion*—Jesus responded to the centurion's request to come heal a servant; he believed Jesus could heal with just a word. *Luke 7:11–15, a widow who lost her only son*—Jesus noticed a funeral procession in Nain, had compassion on the widow, and raised her son; the crowd feared Jesus and glorified God. *John 4:4–10, a Samaritan woman*—Jesus met her in Samaria at the well where she drew water; He showed her sin to her; she believed on Him and told others. *John 5:2, 5–9, a lame man*—Jesus found him waiting for help at the Pool of Bethesda; Jesus healed him; the man testified of Jesus.
2. (a) He tells His followers they reflect His light to the world. They need to show that light boldly, not hide it or be ashamed of it, so God would be glorified. (b) Personal answers. (These acts can give you an opportunity to share about how Christ loves you.)
3. (a) To be His ambassadors in the world. (We are now the ones who carry the gospel to all those Jesus loves and died to save.) (b) We have the heavy responsibility to plead with people to respond to Jesus' salvation. He paid the full price for sin, and we just need to send out the invitations. It should be on our minds in every relationship. We don't want anyone to miss the Good News.
4. That God will supply all the power for their witness. He also assumed they would carry out this important task ("You shall be witnesses to me").
5. They spoke with pure hearts before God, not to please people, but because they were given this task by God. They were also gentle, affectionately longing for the Thessalonians to know the gospel. And they shared their own lives, not just empty words, because they loved those people. They did not consider it an evangelistic project, but a labor of love.
6. We are like a fragrance, diffusing the knowledge of God wherever we are.
7. Personal answers.

LESSON 2

1. Each animal was unique and created after its kind, but humans were made in God's image and likeness.
2. God gave Adam (representing mankind) dominion over all the earth. It wasn't simply that mankind is smarter than animals. God created Adam and Eve in His own image, different from the animals. God also gave them a position of dominance over all other living things on earth, which was under His own total dominance of everything. The man and woman were to fill the earth and

subdue it. All of this gave mankind a unique relationship with God that His other created beings do not have.

3. *Gen. 2:7*—God formed man and breathed life into him. *Gen. 2:8–9*—God gave man a beautiful garden, planted with food and the tree of knowledge of good and evil. *Gen. 2:15*—God assigned man to tend and keep the Garden. *Gen. 2:16–17*—God commanded man not to eat of one tree. *Gen. 2:18–22*—God made woman and brought her to Adam as his wife and suitable companion.
4. *Eph. 1:4–6*—for us to be holy and without blame before Him in love, to be adopted by Him, to be to the praise of the glory of His grace. *Eph. 1:11–12*—for us to have an inheritance and that we be to the praise of His glory. *Eph. 2:10*—for us to accomplish good works through our personal relationship with Jesus Christ and His power.
5. Adam would be subduing the earth, and the Garden's beauty and produce would glorify God.
6. (a) Her first relationship was with God, her Creator. (b) Her second was with Adam.
7. Satan used two methods. First he created doubt to cause Eve to question God's instructions. Then he stirred in Eve a longing for a position she was not created to have.
8. When sin entered the world, the man and woman left their perfect relationship with God and began to think about themselves and honoring themselves more than Him. They had been created for God's glory but were seeking their own glory. When self-centeredness entered, they also tried to declare their own innocence and to blame someone else, which left a rift in their relationship.
9. With the first sin by Adam came the penalty of death, not just for him but for all humanity. So through Adam came the curse of death on everyone.
10. *Rom. 3:10–18*—They are unrighteous and lack understanding, do not seek God but turn aside, and are unprofitable/worthless. *Rom. 5:6, 10*—They are ungodly enemies of God. *Eph. 2:12*—They are separated from God, are excluded from His promises and covenants, and are without hope. (These verses reflect what is true of every unbeliever, regardless of how sweet, kind, and nice a person seems. Why? Because unbelievers have rejected the purpose of their creation.)
11. God's creation speaks to His power and divine nature, but godless people suppress what He clearly reveals. So, while they inherited sin, they also reject the provision to know God in a personal way, because they refuse to accept the clues God put in the world.
12. (a) They are full of wickedness, evil, greed, depravity, envy, murder, strife, deceit, malice; they are gossips, slanderers, God-haters, insolent, arrogant, boastful; they are disobedient to parents, ruthless, senseless, faithless, and heartless. (This list comes from the NIV.) (b) Every one of these character flaws hinders or disrupts true relationships. (Each one shows a love for self and disdain for others. Each is the opposite of what God commands us to be.)
13. *John 3:16–18—Jesus' part:* He offers restoration and salvation; *our part:* we simply believe. *Rom. 5:8–10—Jesus' part:* He died for us, although we have never deserved His mercy; He promises us He will save us from His wrath; *our part:* we accept justification through His blood. *Rom. 10:9–10—God's part:* He raised Jesus from the dead (accepting Jesus' payment for our sin); *our part:* we

simply believe in Jesus' death, burial, and resurrection, which results in our being saved, or justified in God's eyes; then we can also confess our faith and salvation.

14. *Heb. 7:25*—We are saved completely; He intercedes, or prays, for us. *Col. 1:13–14*—We are rescued from darkness and brought into Christ's Kingdom. We are redeemed, or bought back, from the penalty of sin and given full forgiveness. *1 Pet. 2:9–10*—We are a chosen people, royal priesthood, holy nation, and God's special possession; we are now the people of God, who have obtained mercy. He restores us to Him so we can fulfill our purpose: to declare His praises.
15. *Rom. 12:9–21*—Be sincere, devoted to others in love, hospitable, faithful in prayer, joyful in hope, and patient in trials; do good to enemies, hate evil, love good, share with those in need, honor others above yourself, bless people who hate you, rejoice or mourn in sympathy with others, love all people, don't repay evil, don't take revenge, and don't be proud. *Gal. 5:22–26*—Bear the fruit of the Spirit: love, joy, peace, long-suffering, kindness, goodness, faithfulness, gentleness, and self-control, and don't provoke others or envy them. *Matt. 5:43–44*—Love your enemies, bless them, do good to people who hate you, and pray for them. (We may not have a good relationship with someone who hates us, but if we practice these commands, we will please Jesus and may diffuse some of the animosity pointed at us. If we follow these commands through God's power, our relationships will change dramatically, not just with the unsaved, but with everyone. Consider printing these verses, handing out copies, and asking the women to circle each word that talks about how to treat others.)
16. Love. (We should not live for selfish goals or reasons but to glorify God.)

LESSON 3

1. "Leave" parents, "be joined" together, "become one flesh."
2. To be fruitful, multiply, fill the earth, and have dominion over living things on the earth.
3. *Abraham*—lied about Sarah; *Jacob*—lied, cheated, deceived, stole his brother's inheritance, and caused his brother's hatred and desire to kill Jacob; *Tamar*—after being deceived by her father-in-law, tricked him into prostitution and incest; *Rahab*—had been a prostitute before she turned in faith to Jehovah; *David*—let lust rule him and committed adultery (which later led to murder and a cover-up).
4. Mary was a virgin and highly favored by God. The Lord was with her. She found favor with God.
5. She asked honest questions about this announcement but did not seem to doubt the angel's word. She expressed her trust in the Lord and declared herself His servant. She was willing to say yes to this amazing but inconvenient and scary announcement.
6. She praises Him as her Savior, rejoices in God, and praises God as holy and herself as a humble servant. She remembers His past deeds of mercy to Abraham and his descendants, and she recalls that He fulfills His promises.
7. Joseph obeyed the angel, marrying Mary rather than punishing her, and he refrained from physical intimacy with her until after Jesus was born.

8. In response to an angel's warning, Joseph took Mary and Jesus to Egypt, leaving his home to obey God.
9. Herod had all the baby boys killed. If Joseph had not obeyed God, Jesus could have been killed.
10. He explained that He thought they would know He needed to tend to His Father's work.
11. He went back to His home with Mary and Joseph and increased in wisdom, stature, and favor with God and men.
12. (a) Jesus, His mother, and His disciples were at the wedding. (b) Jesus' mother, brothers, and disciples traveled with Him.
13. (a) His own people (in some translations, such as the NIV, "his family") came to stop Him because they thought He was out of His mind. (b) His brothers said Jesus should leave Galilee, go to Judea, and become a public figure. They said He should show His works to the world, not just to His disciples. But his brothers themselves didn't believe Jesus.
14. The Pharisees are misusing a Biblical command for their own benefit. They claim to devote "their money to the Lord," but they are just refusing to provide that money for their own elderly parents, as the law intended.
15. Jesus transferred care of His mother to John, His beloved disciple. Jesus knew John's heart and that he would care for Mary.
16. Jesus explained that it was time to be doing God's work and that His family were those who obeyed God and His Word. This was an unusual stance, since family was so important in Jesus' culture and to Him personally.
17. God. (If a time comes when people might choose between God and family, their relationship with God is the more important one. The Biblical statement compares our love for God to love for all others: we love God so much that all other loves are as hate. This principle could be seen when parents don't want their children to serve in ministry after God has called them. Or when someone in the family asks a person to do something ungodly. Or when people set aside a dear but ungodly relationship because it leads them away from Christ.)
18. Salvation, regeneration, the renewing of the Holy Spirit, justification, and heirship.

LESSON 4

1. Out of Jesus' many disciples, He called twelve to be His apostles, or messengers.
2. Some were unwilling to follow Jesus when He taught hard things. Others knew He was the only true Messiah and should be followed no matter what He taught.
3. Possible answers: You are blessed when you are mocked and spoken evil of because you represent Christ. You should rejoice when you are persecuted falsely for Christ's sake. You should continue in good works that Christ does through you to glorify your Father in Heaven. The Word of God is the ultimate standard for life, and the Law and Prophets will be fulfilled to the last letter.
4. True followers continue to do His will as seen in His Word, and they love one another.
5. *Simon,* whom Jesus named Peter; *Andrew,* Peter's brother; *James,* son of

Zebedee; *John,* another son of Zebedee; *Philip; Matthew,* a tax collector; *Bartholomew; Thomas* (later known as doubting Thomas); *James,* the son of Alphaeus; *Simon,* called the Zealot; *Thaddeus* (a.k.a. Judas, the son of James; a.k.a. Lebbaeus); *Judas Iscariot,* who became a traitor.

6. He spoke to the general public in parables, but He spoke to His disciples more plainly and explained truths to them. (This principle shows that those who desire to closely follow Jesus will always know Him more intimately. He does not reveal important truths to be cast aside. He gives more understanding to those who have a heart to know and love Him.)
7. Jesus isn't afraid of being betrayed. He separates from the crowds because He wants to teach His disciples privately. His death is on a heavenly timetable. (Many translations use the word "because" at the beginning of verse 31. Jesus wanted to explain the chain of events to His disciples so they would understand what was happening.)
8. Power over unclean spirits and the ability to heal all kinds of sicknesses.
9. Peter refuses to accept that Jesus will die. Peter rebukes Jesus for explaining how His death and resurrection will come to pass.
10. After explaining His great agony and sorrow to them, Jesus asks them to pray. But when He returns, they are asleep—not once but twice. (They could not stay awake to carry His heaviest burden, yet He would soon carry their burden of sin on the cross.)
11. When the guards came for Jesus and it was obvious He would not fight back, every disciple left Him and ran away. (All His closest friends—whom He had led, fed, traveled with, taught, loved, and cared for—fled for their lives.)
12. A true friend sharpens us, which means more than being entertaining or comfortable to be around. (A true friend will point out our weaknesses, ungodly attitudes and responses, or other problems she sees. She will do it in love because she cares.)
13. Personal answers.
14. That even if everyone else left Jesus, Peter would be a true friend and stick by Him. (He boasted in Luke 22:33 that he would go with Jesus to prison and death).
15. He went away and wept bitterly.
16. Judas would betray Jesus and turn Him over to them for thirty pieces of silver.
17. He confronted Judas with the reality that He knew his plan before he even carried it out and that He would not stop it. (Jesus emphasized that Judas would betray Him with a kiss, the mark of friendship and brotherly affection.)
18. He recognized that he had betrayed an innocent man, returned the money, and took his own life.
19. Jesus asked the disciples to follow His example and take the lowly servant position among the brethren. His example included humbly serving those who would later deny, betray, and forsake Him.
20. At the time of Jesus' arrest, Peter ran away and denied Jesus. But in Acts 5 Peter stands boldly proclaiming the message of salvation. Even after being arrested and spending the night in prison, Peter boldly speaks to the

authorities and says the disciples will obey God rather than men. (The Holy Spirit living within these men changed them from the inside out.)

LESSON 5

1. *Luke 5; 15*—sitting and eating with sinners; *John 5*—healing a lame man on the Sabbath; *Matt. 12*—healing a blind, mute man and casting demons from him.
2. The Pharisees called him a blasphemer.
3. Jesus healed the paralyzed man to show He had supernatural power.
4. The Pharisees were watching and waiting for a reason to accuse and condemn Jesus. This is a predictable action for critics in general. Once they have decided someone is wrong, they ignore any positive actions and look for more reasons to accuse and condemn the person.
5. Indignant.
6. To try to trick Jesus into a response that could get Him in trouble with the Roman authorities.
7. He told them to give the government what was due to the government and to God what was God's.
8. (a) They gathered a council and plotted to kill Jesus. (b) They did not want to lose their position. They feared the Romans would come and take away their authority and their nation if Jesus continued to gain popularity.
9. Jesus strongly condemns the Pharisees because they are spiritual rulers leading people astray.
10. The heart. Evil, or defilement, comes from the heart. External things are not what actually defiles people.
11. *Matt. 23:3–5*—They tell others to obey laws that they don't obey; they put external symbols of God's Word on their robes to look spiritual; they do things only to get glory from others. *Matt. 23:6–7*—They love to be honored and looked up to by people, to be given the best seats of honor and called Rabbi or teacher. *Matt. 23:23*—They pay their tithe but do not practice justice, mercy, or faithfulness. *Matt. 23:25–26*—They clean up their appearance but continue with sinful actions like extortion and self-indulgence. *Matt. 23:27–28*—They look good outside but are lawless and hypocritical in their hearts. (God saw the hearts of these religious leaders and called them out specifically.)
12. Chief priests, scribes, Judas, elders of the people.
13. That Jesus was perverting the nation, forbidding people to pay taxes to Caesar, and declaring Himself king. (He specifically instructed people to pay taxes to Caesar, so they knew that was a lie.)
14. Herod, his men of war (soldiers), and Pilate.
15. They preferred to honor Caesar than to accept Jesus for Who He was and Who He had proved Himself to be.
16. Jesus willingly suffered the abuse of the trial and crucifixion to accomplish God's greater goal of salvation. (Because of God's sovereignty, all suffering has a purpose, but it often remains unknown to the sufferer.)
17. Personal answers. (We can respond to criticism with anger, justification, excuses, or complaints or with patience, endurance, humility, or introspection. It is easy to respond in the wrong way initially.)

18. With love and forgiveness to every one of His enemies.
19. To love enemies and do good to them. (Although this is the opposite of our natural inclination, it can show God's supernatural love to others.)

LESSON 6

1. Personal answers. (The Bible teaches that while we were still sinners Christ died for us. Although believers realize they are sinners and needed salvation, some were saved when they were young and never really lived a life of debauchery, so it is harder to grasp this concept. Others were on a destructive path when Christ saved them, and they understand His grace more fully. But all of us were saved from God's wrath toward us because of our sin.)
2. Jesus asked Matthew to follow Him. Then Jesus went home with Matthew and ate with him and his friends.
3. The Pharisees wondered why Jesus would associate with sinners.
4. Jesus made it clear that His purpose on earth was to call sinners. He reached out to those who knew they needed a Savior, not to those trusting in their religious actions to get them to Heaven.
5. They accused the woman of being caught in the act of adultery. They said she should be stoned according to the law.
6. Jesus asked them to consider their own hearts. If they were sinless, they could throw the first stone at the woman.
7. First, He did not condemn her. He admonished her to go and sin no more. (Interestingly, John 3:17 mentions that Christ did not come into the world to condemn the world but that through Him people might be saved.)
8. Zacchaeus is described as a rich chief tax collector, probably an important position in a city like Jericho. It would mean the other tax collectors were under him, which is probably why he was rich. But he was also short, and he wanted to see Jesus, so he was willing to climb a tree and wait for Jesus to pass by.
9. When Jesus saw Zacchaeus and asked him to come down so Jesus could stay at his house, Zacchaeus responded immediately and joyfully. But his heart apparently changed as well, because he was willing to restore all the ill-gotten gain from his profession. Jesus said salvation had come to Zacchaeus's house that day.
10. The Pharisees again complained about Jesus spending time with sinners.
11. Jesus did. He asked the woman for a drink of water.
12. They wondered why Jesus was talking with a woman.
13. The woman believed in Jesus, she told her story to her town, and many other people believed in Him.
14. He wore no clothes. He had been chained and kept under guard but had broken free and lived in the wilderness among the tombs.
15. To return to his home and tell people about what God had done for him and the wonderful transformation that had happened.
16. Simon appeared angry and embarrassed by the woman's intrusion. He thought Jesus should have avoided her, since she was sinful.
17. That although both debtors were forgiven, the one whose greater debt was forgiven would love more than the one with less debt. Jesus wanted Simon

to understand that everyone needs Jesus' forgiveness but that not everyone knows the amount of debt Jesus has forgiven that person.

18. The sinful woman was very aware of her sin and Jesus' grace in forgiving it. She was overflowing in praise and gratitude to the point that she would pour out her most expensive possession on Him just to honor him. The Pharisee thought he was important and deserved to have Jesus in his home. He did not feel an obligation even to wash Jesus' feet or honor Him with a kiss of welcome.
19. Foolish, disobedient, deceived, serving various lusts and pleasures, living in malice and envy, hateful and hating one another. (The list of sins might not seem to fit us exactly, but we were certainly all disobedient to God and going our own way. Romans 3:10 says that none are righteous—not even one.)

LESSON 7

1. (a) Jesus was grieving the death of John the Baptist. (b) The people followed Jesus because He could heal the sick. Although He was grieving, He had compassion for their needs and healed their sick.
2. He taught in the synagogues of Galilee, proclaimed the Good News, and healed every disease and sickness among the people.
3. The centurion asks to have his servant healed because he is paralyzed and suffering. Jesus speaks the word, and the servant is healed without Jesus even seeing the servant in person.
4. The man was covered in leprosy, a terrible disease for which there was no cure. (It was considered contagious, so lepers were to live separate from the population; and when they passed anyone, they had to announce they were unclean. The effects of the disease, and the nerve endings it damaged, meant lepers could not feel pain. This resulted in ugly sores and disfigurement from damage to their appendages.)
5. Jesus healed the centurion's servant from afar. He could have healed the leper the same way, but in great compassion, Jesus healed the leper by touching him.
6. *Matt. 15:32*—Jesus saw that the people had been following Him for three days and were hungry, so He cared about their physical needs and wanted to feed them. *Matt. 20:30–34*—Jesus had compassion on two blind men who wanted to see. Although the crowd had rebuked them, Jesus had compassion and healed them, and they followed Him. *Mark 2:5–12*—Jesus showed His power over physical problems to prove His deity. He healed the paralyzed man to show He has power to forgive sins, since both healing and forgiving are supernatural. *Luke 7:11–13*—Jesus saw the funeral of a man whose mother was a widow. Jesus' heart went out to her. He raised the young man from the dead and gave him to his mother. (All these show Jesus' tender heart.)
7. His son was close to death, so the man came to ask Jesus to heal his son. Jesus told the man to go home and that his son would live.
8. In total faith in Jesus' words, the official left. On his way home, his servants came to tell him that his son was healed. The man realized that the moment Jesus spoke, the fever left his son. This miracle caused the man's whole household to believe in Jesus.
9. *Ps. 113:4–7*—Even though the Lord reigns over all, He stoops to look on the heavens and earth; He raises the poor from the dust; He lifts the needy from

the ash heap. *Prov. 31:8–9*—God commands His people to speak up for the needy and destitute and to defend their rights.

10. To love like Jesus. (This means laying down our lives for others and meeting their material needs. We are not to pity them, as in feeling sorry for them, but are to have true compassion, like Jesus did, and meet their needs.)
11. Love the Lord your God with all your heart, and love your neighbor as yourself.
12. The Jewish man who was stripped, beaten, and needy; the priest who went by; the Levite who went by; and the Samaritan who stopped to help.
13. Samaritans were considered outcasts by Jews and were looked down on. There was bad blood between the groups, like racial tension. A Samaritan had no reason to help a Jew.
14. The Samaritan got dirty, used his own oil and wine to help, gave up his donkey to let the man ride to the inn, spent time, spent money on the man for the innkeeper to keep him, and said he would return and pay more if necessary. He could not have done more if the injured man had been his best friend or relative, but he was a stranger.
15. Sell all his possessions, give to the poor (which would give him treasure in Heaven), then follow Jesus.
16. The rich man was sad. He loved his possessions more than he loved Jesus, so he left unforgiven.
17. They are without hope because they are without God. (To be separate from God—the one relationship every person was created to experience—is to be hopeless in this world and for eternity.)
18. To set Christ as their Lord and be ready to gently and respectfully share the truth and the reason for their hope.
19. "Great love," "rich in mercy," "grace," "incomparable riches of his grace." (He wants to show us His incomparable grace and kindness through offering us the free gift of salvation.)
20. Jesus is the ultimate answer of hope that every person needs. (Sometimes people have other needs so they can see the love of God in action as those needs are met. But their ultimate need is Jesus.)

LESSON 8

1. (a) Taught, proclaimed the good news, healed diseases and sicknesses. (b) Personal answers. (The crowds followed Jesus because of His healing ministry.)
2. Jesus had compassion on His followers. (He did not look at them as a group of followers who would bring Him fame and glory. He looked at them as needy people.)
3. People came from Galilee; Judea, including Jerusalem, Idumea; regions around the Jordan; and around Tyre and Sidon. (Tyre and Sidon were Phoenician cities on the Mediterranean; Perea was a region east of the Jordan River.)
4. Jesus' popularity must have spread through word of mouth. The people followed Him wherever He went.
5. Jesus preached the Word to the people.
6. It was evidence of Jesus' deity and would verify His message.

7. At first the people were amazed at His teachings, and He was glorified by all. They marveled at His gracious words.
8. The crowd was angry when Jesus said He would not be doing the same miracles in His hometown as in other places. He had not received the same honor in His hometown as elsewhere. The people changed from praising and honoring Him to trying to kill Him.
9. The people were following Jesus to get something they wanted. They followed Him, not because they understood He was the Messiah, but rather because they wanted Him to heal their sick and perform other miracles for them. (This was true not just in Jesus' day. Many people are interested in following Jesus when they want something from Him. Jesus asks all people to follow Him because of Who He is, not what He can do for them.)
10. They declared they wanted Him crucified. These were the same crowds that had followed Jesus and had sung His praises.
11. That He is the bread of life, that He satisfies spiritual hunger and thirst, that He won't cast out any who come to Him, and that He came to do the Father's will. (Jesus came from Heaven to do not His own will but the Father's. It is God's will that everyone who believes in the Son of God will have everlasting life.)
12. Some doubt the truth of Jesus' statement because they have wrong presuppositions. They complain about Jesus' remark that He has come from Heaven, because they think Joseph was His father.
13. That those who believe in Him have everlasting life and that He is the living bread and they need to partake of that bread to have life, because He is giving His life or His flesh for the world.
14. They are confused because they think He is talking about physically giving them His flesh to eat.
15. They leave Jesus. (They were not true disciples who were willing to learn and try to understand Jesus. So when things got tough, they gave up and left.)
16. Some said Jesus was a good man, while others said He deceived people. Some admired His teaching, which showed He had great learning. Others said they knew where He was from, so He couldn't be Messiah.
17. Much of the seed that was sown fell in places where it did not grow or soon died. However, because the seed had been sown broadly, some fell on good soil. It grew and produced a large crop. This represents sharing the gospel. Sowing the Word in large groups will fall on rocky and thorny soil, but some will fall on the ears of people willing to listen and believe.
18. When Jesus was alone with His disciples, He explained things to them in more detail.

LESSON 9

1. To pray to the Lord of the harvest and ask Him to send workers into His harvest field.
2. He decided they would leave town. He had spent time praying and knew His purpose for coming to earth. Rather than letting the tyranny of the urgent or people's desires for Him dictate to Him, Jesus let His mission dictate where He went and what He did.
3. Not to do My own will, but "the will of Him who sent Me."

4. He prayed that the Father might remove the difficult path in front of Him—the pain and agony of crucifixion—but He was committed to the Father's will over His own.
5. He made Himself nothing. He took on the form of a servant, submitting Himself to human form, being obedient to the point of death.
6. These are the resources Jesus left: *John 15:14–15*—The revelation of all the things from His Father. *John 16:13–14*—The Spirit of truth, Who would guide them in all truth. The Spirit also would reveal the Father's message, since it was the same as the Son's. *John 17:8–9*—God's words to His followers. They received them as God's words. He also declared that He prayed for them and all those who believe on Him. (Jesus was preparing His followers to carry on His mission after He left earth. He wanted each one to also be committed to do the Father's will, and He gave them all the means to understand God's will.)
7. Personal answers. (Answers should include listening to God and hearing His voice.)
8. How well He knew the Father.
9. Through Christ, Who gave him strength.
10. That the gospel itself is the power of God to salvation. It is not the presentation of the gospel that is powerful or the messenger that needs to be powerful. The gospel itself has the power to change lives and must simply be presented.
11. (a) Without God, we can do nothing. (It is easy to forget this principle when we spend time planning, preparing, and outlining our plans to serve God or minister to others. Sometimes those plans take precedence over seeking God's power and depending on Him. Sometimes we don't even consult God about His will but jump ahead with our own plans.) (b) Jesus relied totally on the Father throughout His life on earth. Jesus did not seek His own way, but always sought the Father's will.
12. Love the Lord your God with all your heart, soul, and mind. (It seems like a simple command at first glance. And if we would have that mindset—that our whole heart, soul, and mind are totally devoted to God—we would never try to go our own way or usurp His authority. But our affection for God is often overshadowed by our affection for our own way and for things of the world.)
13. To really know God, you must believe in Jesus. (If you reject Jesus and His claims, you have rejected God as well. And you will not know Scripture, because it testifies to the truth of Jesus' claims. Many religious groups claim to know God, but they reject Jesus' deity and refuse to believe that His death, burial, and resurrection must be accepted for someone to have eternal life.)
14. When we seek approval from other people, we might be tempted to follow the person with the best presentation or the loudest voice or the biggest crowd or the one whose message is the most palatable to us. But if we follow God, we must follow only the One He sent, not one of our own choosing. Following Jesus, Who claims to be the only way to God, in a pluralistic society will often incur ridicule or scorn. Following Jesus, Who says to love our enemies and give our goods to the poor, seems counterintuitive to secular thinking. But Jesus is the only one God sent for us to believe in.)
15. I do nothing of myself; I always do those things that please Him.
16. "I have glorified You on the earth." (Jesus always did the Father's will, so Jesus

only had to complete the things the Father had given Him to do. Not everything in the world was set right, but He completed the mission God had given Him to accomplish.)

17. To finish his race with joy. (That meant finishing the ministry he had received from the Lord.)
18. Personal answers. (Each person has a unique purpose that God wants him or her to fulfill. This includes relationships He wants that person to have, ministries He wants that person to do, words He wants that person to say. No one has to fulfill all the tasks in the world, but if a person is constantly seeking the tasks that God has for him or her, and is willing to do whatever God asks, that person will be able to finish those things with God's strength.)